INSTILL & INSPIRE

INSTILL

INSPIRE

The John & Vivian Hewitt Collection of African-American Art

TEXT BY
GRACE C. STANISLAUS

UNIVERSITY OF PITTSBURGH PRESS

Published by the University of Pittsburgh Press, Pittsburgh, Pa., 15260

Manufactured in Canada
Printed on acid-free paper

FIRST EDITION
10 9 8 7 6 5 4 3 2 1

ISBN 13: 978-0-8229-4504-8
ISBN 10: 0-8229-4504-5

Cataloging-in-Publication data is available from the Library of Congress

JACKET ART: Romare Bearden, *Homage to Mary Lou,* 1984. Lithograph on paper, 29 × 20 in. Art © Romare Bearden Foundation / Licensed by VAGA, New York, NY.

JACKET & BOOK DESIGN: Joel W. Coggins

To my mother and father Christine and the late Myron Cook, who gifted me with love, direction, correction, and life itself, without which there can be neither art nor the love of it.

To Vivian and the late John Hewitt, whose passion and commitment to the African American community, as well as their support for both renowned and emerging artists, resulted in a powerful collection of black works now made available to the world through its magnificent home at the Gantt Center for African-American Arts + Culture in Charlotte, North Carolina.

To collectors of African American art, without whose acquisitions true artists would doubtless continue to create—ah, but because of these collectors, the many communities that the works inhabit are enriched profoundly and immeasurably.

YVONNE C. COOK

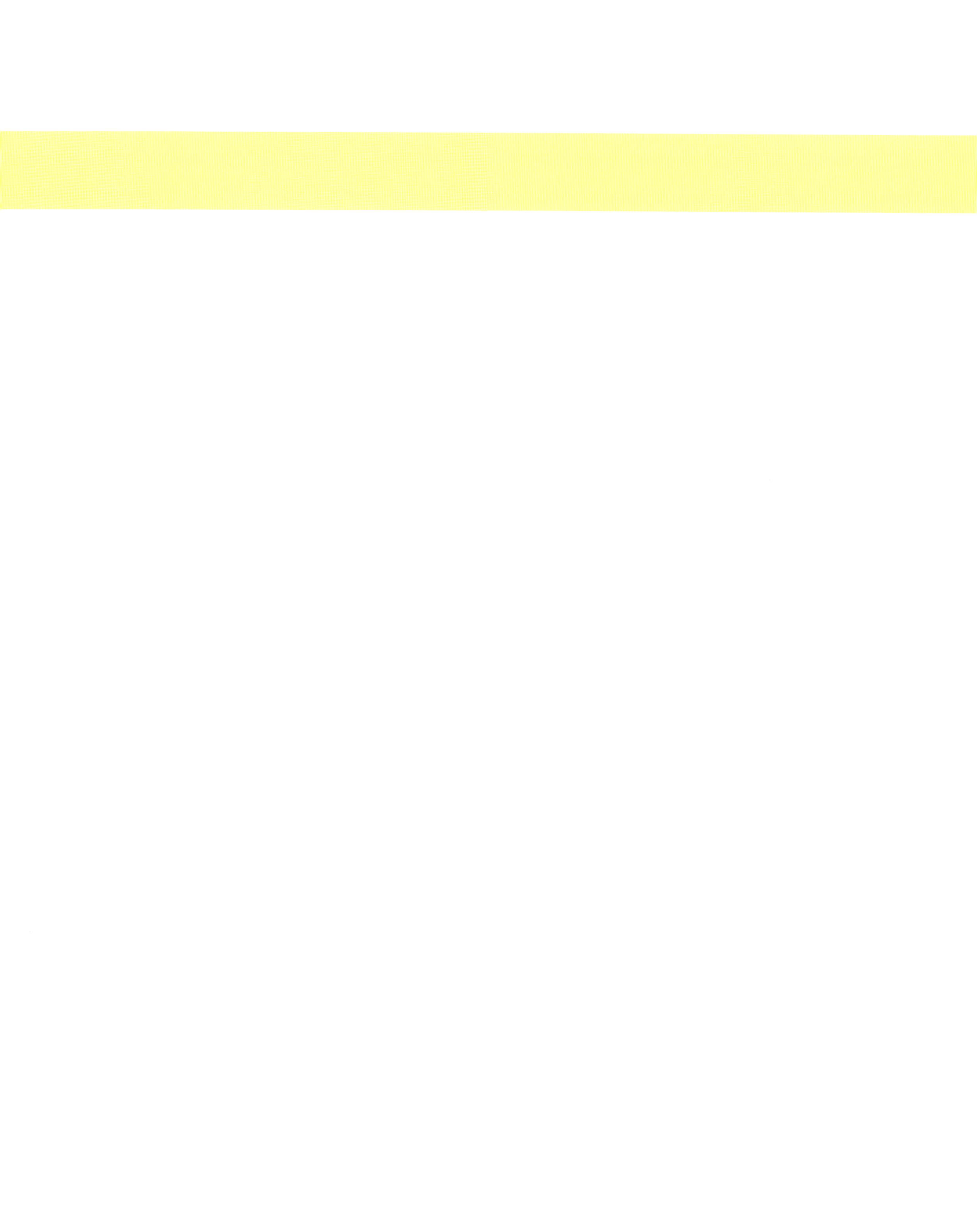

CONTENTS

FOREWORD

THE SOCIAL & CULTURAL CONSCIOUSNESS OF COLLECTING & EXHIBITING AFRICAN AMERICAN VISUAL ART

Throughout five decades John and Vivian Hewitt, both scholars, followed a vision of collecting and living with African American visual arts that deeply enriched their careers and their lives. They were extremely fortunate to be living in New York in the early 1950s, when they began the adventure of acquiring art reflecting the culture, life, challenges, and heritage of numerous professional African American artists. Both of them considered art to be the spirit of life, yet when they reflected upon other existing collections in museums and civic centers, they found that many failed to reflect the cross-cultural richness of New York, its history, and its story. It was clear that major museums, cultural centers, galleries, educational institutions, most libraries, churches, and exhibitions chose not to adequately recognize the phenomenal visual arts of African Americans and their contributions to American culture and history.

Established African American artists, collectors, and some galleries in New York served as beacons of light in helping the Hewitts grasp the historical significance and current scope of the lives and contributions of African American artists in New York and nationally. They networked with the staffs of galleries and institutions to locate and incorporate into their lives contemporary artists who were currently working with these organizations as well as many living artists who had produced art as part of the WPA period in New York. Through carefully prioritizing their resources, John and Vivian Hewitt were able to travel throughout the United States, the Caribbean, and the Americas and collect works of master artists who are included in their incredible collection, described in this publication.

THE HEWITTS' ROLE AS COLLECTORS

While John and Vivian were meeting hundreds of artists and attending numerous museum and gallery receptions it was clear to them that the majority of African American artists lacked the kind of support network that was essential in helping enhance their careers and visibility. One can collect art, but that does not help the artist in the long run if others are also not collecting. When the Hewitts traveled throughout the country they reflected upon the numerous art collectors they knew and who were incorporating African American art in their personal and museum collections.

John and Vivian Hewitt's level of social interest and passion for art inspired them to open their home to potential collectors, sponsors, and artists to visit and network with one another. They met many incredible people who had not visited a home with the range of cross-cultural art with an emphasis on African American art that the Hewitts had in theirs. Such visitors immediately related to the depth of their collection. I am sure that the Hewitts could feel the energy flowing from many of the visitors, including artists, as they had never given themselves permission to collect art reflecting their own cultural history and heritage. Vivian and the late John Hewitt were models as teachers, coaches, and catalysts by having in-depth discussions, and soon they also became collectors of African American art both regional and national.

It became clear to the Hewitts that the purpose of sharing their collection with others was to enhance the visibility and perceptions of artists who were descendants of the African Diaspora for their cultural contributions to this nation. To this end, they decided that it was vital to keep the collection intact, to assure that it would always be available to others to view and learn to understand the depth of their legacy. Fortunately, through the foresight of Hugh McColl, chairman and CEO, Bank of America and its foundation acquired the Hewitt Collection of African American Art and bequeathed it as a gift to the Afro-American Cultural Center now known as the Harvey B. Gantt Center for African-American Arts + Culture in Charlotte, North Carolina.

JONATHAN GREEN
Artist and Curator, The Vibrant Vision Collection
Managed by Jonathan Green Studios, LLC

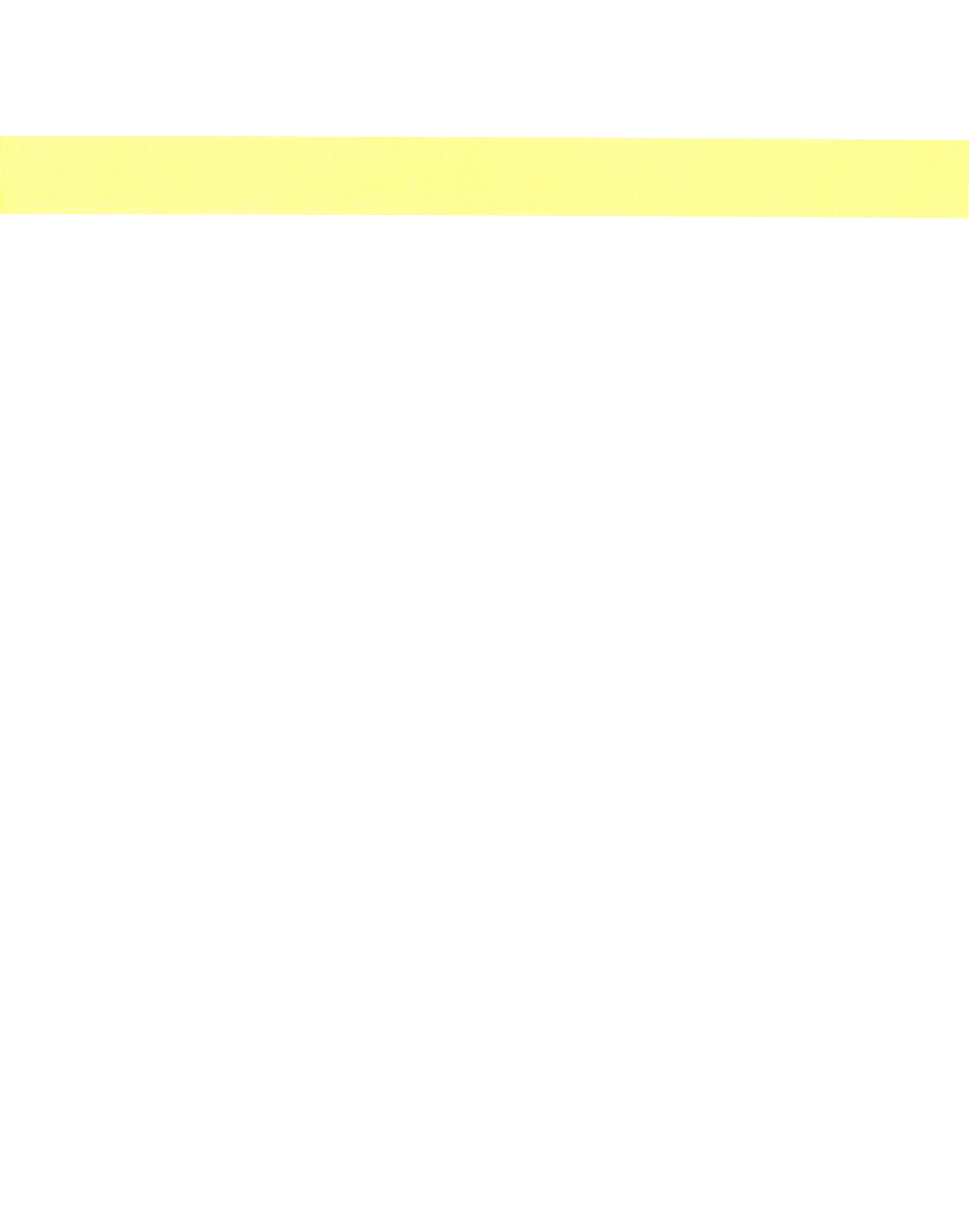

ACKNOWLEDGMENTS

Through the depictions and accounts of the art presented in these pages, this book demanded to be published. I was simply fortunate enough to obey the command.

Of course, the several people who played both major and supportive roles directly in the book's preparation have earned my everlasting gratitude. First and foremost, these include the authorial team comprised of essay writer Grace Stanislaus and the writer of the foreword, Jonathan Green, as well as Ervin Dyer and Bethany Miga, who contributed the section devoted to the collectors. The words of these brilliant writers dance off the pages.

Their prose was beautifully and contextually augmented by the observations of the Harvey B. Gantt Center president and CEO David Taylor. He and COO Bonita Buford, assistant registrar Alexys Taylor, and former registrar Caroline Manning were indispensable to productive interactions with the Gantt. The wherewithal of the Gantt Center to anchor its collections with the Hewitt artworks was made possible by the philanthropy of Bank of America. I extend many thanks to the Charlotte angels.

I shall always be grateful to both the leadership and staff of the University of Pittsburgh Press, who provided expert guidance, collaboration, and professionalism throughout the process of moving the enterprise from ambitious idea to publication; to Tracy Myers, whose overall and curatorial support were of monumental importance; and to Kathy Wilson Humphrey, who, as senior vice-chancellor, infused into the project the gravitas of my University of Pittsburgh alma mater.

I am indebted to special people Karen Farmer White and Oliver Byrd for their unwavering friendship expressed in the most meaningful ways, and to Robert Hill, who always rejoices at the intersection of history, art . . . and blackness.

The collectors who generously participated in interviews through which their insights shine are Harriet and Harmon Kelly, MD; Walter O. Evans, MD; and Nancy and the late Milton Washington, all of whose own collections instill and inspire.

As with everything that engages me or that I undertake, I am strengthened and buoyed by my family, all of the Cooks. Thank you, my brothers Myron III and Eddie, nieces Erin and Brieann, and my sister-in-law Valerie. I appreciate all of you being you, and I thank my extended family, too!

Though many heads, hands, and hearts deserve credit for bringing this book to publication, any shortcomings that attach to the book are mine, not theirs. Even so, if fault be found, I hope it does not significantly diminish the aesthetic, educational, and edifying value of the reading and viewing experience of *Instill and Inspire: The Vivian and John Hewitt Collection of African-American Art*.

YVONNE C. COOK
Executive-in-Charge
December 15, 2016

INSTILL & INSPIRE

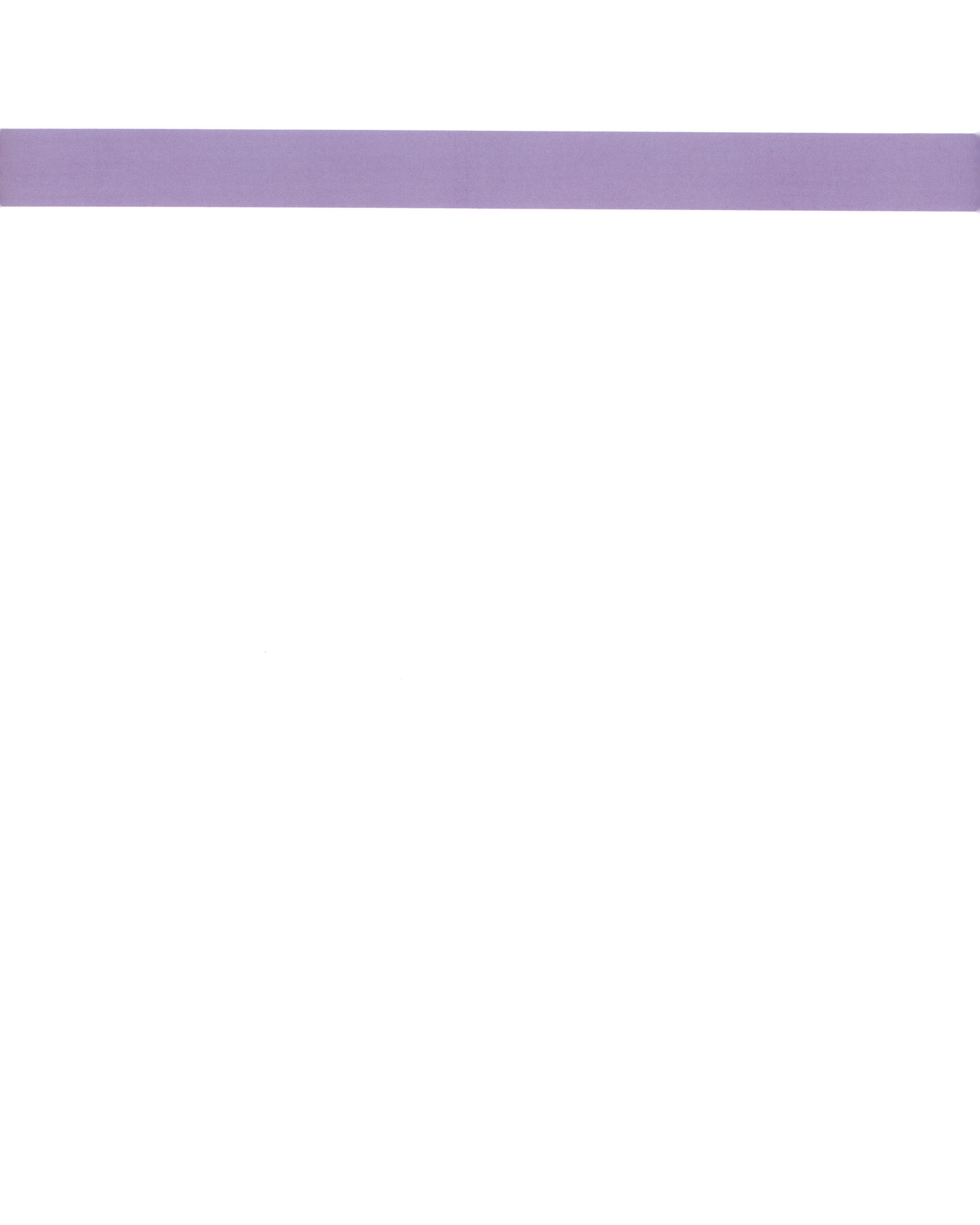

A HISTORICAL NARRATIVE

AFRICAN AMERICAN PATRONAGE OF THE ARTS THROUGH THE LENS OF THE JOHN & VIVIAN HEWITT COLLECTION

GRACE C. STANISLAUS

The richly textured narrative about how the John and Vivian Hewitt Collection was established has already often been told: a young, newly married, African American, professional, middle-class couple directed their love for each other and passion for the arts into the shared purpose of accumulating a major collection of African American art. By positioning their story within the broader narrative arc and intersections of American history, art history, and African American cultural history, one is able to better define its importance as well as spotlight other intricately interwoven stories. One among them is the flourishing over the centuries of a robust system of African American patronage of the arts into which the story of the Hewitt Collection can be contextualized.

Also among the intimately linked stories is the milestone opening of the National Museum of African American History and Culture as part of the Smithsonian Institution on the National Mall in Washington, DC, after a protracted and hard-fought battle; the breakthrough in consciousness that led to the gradual acceptance and valuation of African and African American culture, history, and art; the long-resisted but indisputable truth about the extraordinary contributions of people of African descent to American and world culture; the embedding of black culture in the foundations of American society despite resistance and against all odds; the rise of a postslavery black national identity that was framed around self-empowerment and self-determination and catalyzed by the resistance to segregation, discrimination, and racism; and the once inconceivable dream, so passionately articulated by Martin Luther King Jr., symbolically realized by the two-term election of the first African American president of the United States, Barack Obama.

Within the broader narrative of African American cultural history is embedded a foundational truth about an insidious bipolarity in the thinking, attitudes, and behavioral responses of European Americans toward Africans and people of African descent. It emerged during the annexation and colonization of Africa and further developed during the transatlantic slave trade and slavery in colonial and antebellum America, Brazil, and the Caribbean. And it manifested in full force through the brutalization and dehumanization of Africans and the overt campaign to destroy their art, culture, beliefs, rituals, and traditions. It took many forms, including the devaluation of African peoples and their valuation as commodities in the economic systems of slavery and of postslavery America. From as early as the fifteenth century this bipolarity operated in the interstice between fear, fascination, repulsion, and entrancement with blackness, and although it manifests differently today, it continues in America in the polarized relationship between blacks and whites.

It can also be spotlighted in the efforts of Western missionaries and colonialists to Christianize Africans, which often led to the destruction of objects they deemed paganistic and to the denigration of African peoples and their traditions as uncivilized and barbaric. On the opposite spectrum it generated a fascination and entrancement with African "exoticism" and "primitiveness," with the aesthetic beauty and power of African art and with the physiognomies of African bodies. Consequently, many Western missionaries, collectors, artists, ethnographers, cultural anthropologists, and social "scientists" stole, appropriated, co-opted, used, and abused African peoples and their cultures and objects of art. And, without discrimination, they put both people and objects on display in world's fairs and circuses and in curio cabinets, galleries, and museums.

Western fascination with African primitivism, which in the art world generated major exhibitions like *"Primitivism" in 20th Century Art: Affinity of the Tribal and the Modern* at the Museum of Modern Art, also perpetuated myths that African artists were anonymous and that African peoples lacked the capacity to appreciate or even recognize the aesthetic beauty and value of their objects. These myths girded the notion that the value, valuation, and validation of African art (and peoples) could only be realized through the Western gaze and as a result of the patronage of white Europeans and Americans. They also supported a false construct of black invisibility.

In fact, a robust patronage system existed within many precolonial African societies that by comparison perhaps did not rival the European patronage system in purpose and scale but was certainly comparable in its structure. African kings, chiefs, *obis*, and community members commissioned objects of art for their aesthetic beauty and utility, to appease and communicate with the ancestors, or to protect and enrich the community. As in Europe, favored artists built their reputations and realized their livelihood on this patronage system.

For African artists in the New World the making of art and the centrality of the place of artists within the community are among the many cultural beliefs transported in spirit, memory, and practice during the Middle Passage. Despite the many extraordinary obstacles in their path, including the overt effort to destroy their traditions, art, culture, and heritage, African and African American artists in colonial and postcolonial America continued to create art, though often in secret and away from the gaze of their slave masters and overseers.

In America and elsewhere throughout the African diaspora, the stories most often told are about denial—denial of opportunity and access for African American artists to art academies and salons and to white mainstream museums and galleries. Several artists departed to Europe to find there the support, acceptance, and recognition that were denied them in the United States.

Within the broader narrative of the strained, troubled, and often turbulent relationship of white America with its former slaves are stories about the strength, perseverance, and resiliency that were generated from basic instincts to survive under extreme conditions of brutality and cruelty. Whatever its impetus, it fueled a fire within African Americans that was demonstrated most visibly during periods of resistance and struggle against segregation, discrimination, and racism, and for cultural reclamation and self-determinism. The Pan-African movement, the civil rights movement, the Black Power movement, the Back to Africa movement, the Black Is Beautiful movement, and the Black Lives Matter movement highlight key periods in the struggle for and ascendancy of political, social, economic, and cultural power. They also foreground the emergence of an African-centric, nationalist, black identity that was seen in fashion, style, and dress—in big and well-groomed Afros and dashikis and in raised, clenched fists that confirmed black power and solidarity.

During one extraordinary period in American cultural history an unrestrained explosion of black culture resulted in what is now celebrated as the Harlem Renaissance of the 1920s and 1930s. In the essay "Whose Renaissance Was It Really: Black Art Patronage of the 1920s and 1930s," published in *American University Graduate Review*, Rodney Trapp identifies two types of patrons that supported the surge in private patronage of black artists during the period of the Harlem Renaissance: primitivists and humanists. Trapp posits that a "fascination with the spirit and perceived exoticism of the darker race" led "primitivists" like William E. Harmon and Charlotte Osgood Mason, among others, to covertly and overtly control, influence, and encourage artists toward a neoprimitive style. Archibald Motley Jr. was one among several artists he identified who received acceptance and approval within the mainstream art world as a result of the benevolence of these white patrons.

While the history of European and white American art patronage is fairly well known and documented, less so is the story of the emergence of African American patrons and the history of patronage of African American art and artists. From the era of Western missionaries, abolitionists, and patrons championing Africans and African Americans, to the period of the Harlem Renaissance—when many African American artists relied on the benevolence and noblesse oblige of European American patrons, to the Hewitts' story, a new narrative has emerged. It is historically framed around Alain Locke's call, under the banner of the New Negro movement, to uplift the black race. His call was heeded by white patrons and also taken up by an emerging black middle class and black bourgeoisie. It was fueled by an emergent consciousness and pride in the flourishing of black art and culture throughout the African diaspora despite the fallow soil of slavery in which it was planted. In essence, Locke and others rallied black consciousness under the cry: If not us, then who would recognize, support, and celebrate the achievements of Africans in America and throughout the diaspora?

The narrative about African American patronage of the arts and its precedent in preslavery Africa intersects directly at this point with the Hewitts' story—the story of impassioned collectors who nurtured genuine relationships with artists and valued them as much as the objects they produced. The Hewitts and other collectors—Bernard and Shirley Kinsey, Larry and Brenda Thompson, Harmon and Harriett Kelley, Nancy Washington, Dr. Walter Evans, and Grant Hill, among many others—by virtue of their very existence challenged the historically entrenched and falsely constructed notions about the value of black art being assigned only through the beneficence of white patrons, about African Americans being disinvested from their cultural patrimony, and about the lack of an African American art patronage system.

In describing *Instill and Inspire: The John and Vivian Hewitt Collection of African-American Art*, the exhibition presented at the August Wilson Center for African American Culture in Pittsburgh in 2017 and the basis for this book, it was asserted that the exhibition provides "an exceptional opportunity for Pittsburghers to see first-rate works that will enrich our understanding of African American culture and re-shape our thinking about the value of the arts."

Enrich our understanding of African American culture and re-shape our thinking about the value of the arts. How does positioning the John and Vivian Hewitt story in the arc of history re-shape our thinking and deepen our understanding of the value of African American culture and the arts? What can we learn from how their consciousness was expanded as they moved beyond being mere lovers of art and culture to being avowed and passionate collectors of African American art and then major patrons of the arts within a storied history and tradition that dates back to Africa? Can a deeper understanding of the significance of the acquisition of their collection by a major corporation indeed re-shape our understanding of the value of African American art? How is this all positioned within the context of black art, artists, and culture needing to be and being publicly validated and recognized as part of America's historic trust?

Like the story of the National Museum of African American History and Culture, the story of the Hewitt Collection finding its home at the Harvey B. Gantt Center for African-American Arts + Culture in Charlotte, North Carolina—being cared for, protected, and displayed there for posterity and for public education, enrichment, and enjoyment—marks a milestone event in the ascendance and acceptance of African American art and culture.

As she described how the collection was acquired by Bank of America and toured throughout the United States, Vivian Hewitt referenced the moment as a synergistic alignment of the bank's interest in acquiring a major collection of African American art and their interest in making the Hewitt Collection accessible to the public. In fact, the acquisition of the Hewitt Collection in 1998 at that particular time in history adds another layer to the compelling narrative that highlights how institutional and individual patronage of black art and artists evolved over the centuries. It wasn't just serendipity that led to the acquisition of the collection; it was a moment of historic convergence of the growing awareness and appreciation of black cultural and artistic achievements. While Bank of America's continuing support of the arts is unprecedented in this century, it had its antecedents in previous eras when institutional patrons generated a new level of recognition and support for African American artists, among them the Public Works Art Project of the Works Progress Administration and the Harmon Foundation.

In preserving, supporting, documenting, interpreting, and presenting African American art, culture, and artists, institutions such as the Harmon Foundation, Howard University Gallery of Art, Fisk University/Carl Van Vechten Gallery, Spelman College Museum of Art, Clark Atlanta University Galleries of Art, the DuSable Museum of African American History, the Barnett-Aden Gallery, the Schomburg Center for Research in Black Culture, and the Studio Museum in Harlem, among others, raised to another level consciousness about African American cultural, artistic, social, political, economic, educational, and literary achievements. And in doing so, they also subverted long-held notions of black invisibility and marginality and created an alternate mainstream for black culture that decentered the focus from the white mainstream as the critical entry point. They created another path to the marketplace for black artists. On this new path artists encountered John and Vivian Hewitt, who were members in a still-exclusive club of African American patrons of the arts and who were at the foreground of a newly flourishing African American patronage system.

It must be acknowledged, however, that not every institution got it right in terms of their engagement with African American art and artists. The white-run Harmon Foundation, which was established in 1926 by wealthy real estate developer and philanthropist William E. Harmon (1862–1928) upon the prompting of Alain Locke (1885–1954), a Howard University professor and proponent of the Harlem Renaissance and of the New Negro movement, provided much-needed financial support and access for black artists through its annual cash award prizes and national traveling exhibitions. Hale Woodruff (1900–1980), one of the artists represented in the Hewitt Collection, and Palmer Hayden (1890–1973) were the first recipients of the Fine Arts Award for the Distinguished Achievement among Negroes.

But the foundation was excoriated by no more vocal an advocate for African American art and artists than the celebrated artist, scholar, educator, and Renaissance man Romare Bearden (1911–1988). While he acknowledged its role in supporting artists, which was especially critical during the Depression era, Bearden also called the foundation out and accused it of coddling artists and lowering artistic standards. A major patron of African American art and artists, the foundation was also a business enterprise that marketed, subsidized, and benefited from the sale of the art. In counterpoint to its patronage and benevolence, the paternalistic practice of having primarily white-only juries to select the African American awardees, the undue influence the foundation often exerted on the artist's aesthetic choices, and its control of the market were the symptoms of the bipolarity that was inherent in its culture.

In 1967 the Harmon Foundation gave Fisk University several hundred works of art by African American artists, another milestone event that made the university's Carl Van Vechten Gallery an important site for the study, preservation, documentation, presentation, and appreciation of black art and artists. The year that the Harmon Foundation ceased its operation in 1968, the Studio Museum in Harlem was founded with the mission to collect, preserve, and interpret the art of African Americans and artists of the African diaspora. It marked the passing of the baton and another milestone event in African American cultural history.

In tandem with the establishment of these institutions, the gap in scholarship began to be bridged and closed with the establishment of black studies programs and departments throughout the country and the publication of seminal books and catalogues, including *American Negro Art*, by Cedric Dover; *Two Centuries of Black American Art*, by

David C. Driskell; and *Modern Negro Art*, by James Porter. Over the centuries many other books and articles were published by distinguished historians, scholars, and practitioners Romare Bearden, Robert Farris Thompson, Elsa Honig Fine, Cedric Dover, Samella Lewis, David Driskell, Richard Powell, Kobena Mercer, and Kelly Jones, among others. They rectified the brazen exclusion of African American artists from art history books while establishing a counterpoint to the narrative of black invisibility and healing the spirit and psyche of African American artists. Such a flood of publications correcting the omission of the achievements and contributions of people of African descent to American and world culture was essential as a healing and interventionist strategy against the ongoing devaluation of black culture in all areas of life, politics, sports, the arts, science, education, business, technology, the entertainment industry, and so on. And the combined strategies of self-empowerment that led to the establishment of black educational and cultural institutions and to new publications staunched the poison that had entered both African American and European American consciousness—a transgenerational poison caused and fostered by the lack of recognition, acceptance, awareness, and knowledge of the richness of African American cultural history and heritage.

Along with making regular visits to educational and cultural organizations in Atlanta where they lived and worked and in New York where they eventually settled, John and Vivian Hewitt turned to these books and scholars and referenced them as they educated themselves and became knowledgeable collectors, patrons, and cultural consumers.

In her own words, Vivian Hewitt has described and explained the historical context and climate in which she and her husband John established their place as major patrons of the arts, specifically of African American art and artists. "Art was cheap and we could afford it. That's how we began." To further amplify this statement, it is important to note that African American art was cheap not as a consequence of artists devaluing their work but because at the time they began collecting, with few exceptions, artists were still struggling for access and support and to find a market for their work within and outside of the mainstream art world. "We were committed to supporting African American artists because they were not mainstreamed to the extent white artists were." In fact, the

Hewitts' commitment to and support for the arts extended far beyond the typical interest of collectors and consumers of culture. As deeply engaged patrons of the arts, their home in New York became the nexus and gathering place for intellectuals and artists, an art gallery, and a salon.

"We are an excellent example that you do not have to be rich to love art, to collect art. We mentored other people who were starting their collections. I can't begin to tell you how proud and pleased we are to have young people come up to me and say, 'Mrs. Hewitt, you've inspired me. I'm starting to collect.' And I tell them, 'Don't hesitate. Just do it. Just start.'" In her rallying cry for a younger generation to grab the baton as collectors and patrons of the arts, Vivian Hewitt foregrounds an essential lesson about how African American culture, art, and history will continue to be valued and preserved for the current and future generations.

Ken Lewis, chairman of Bank of America at the time the Hewitt Collection was acquired, notes in the preface to the exhibition catalogue, "Education has always been one of the primary aims of art—education not just of the mind, but of the soul, and not just of individuals, but of whole communities." In his statement and Vivian Hewitt's statements are many of the fundamental truths that underlie the broader narrative of African American cultural history. And embedded within this narrative is the now-legendary story of John and Vivian Hewitt's love for one another and their love affair with African American art and artists.

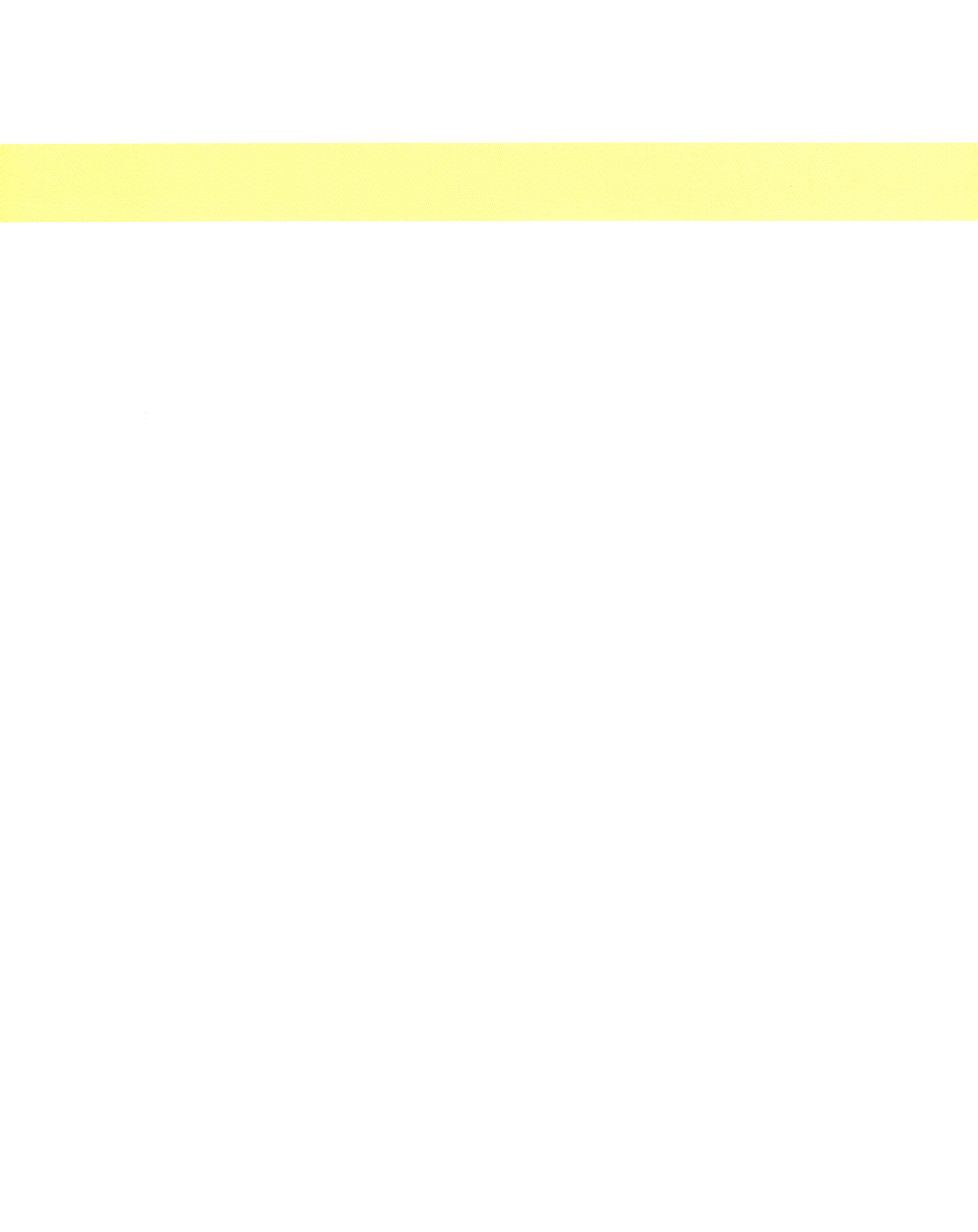

PLATES

CHARLES ALSTON
American, 1907–1977
Woman Washing Clothes, c. 1970
oil pastel on paper
30 ½ × 20 ½ in.

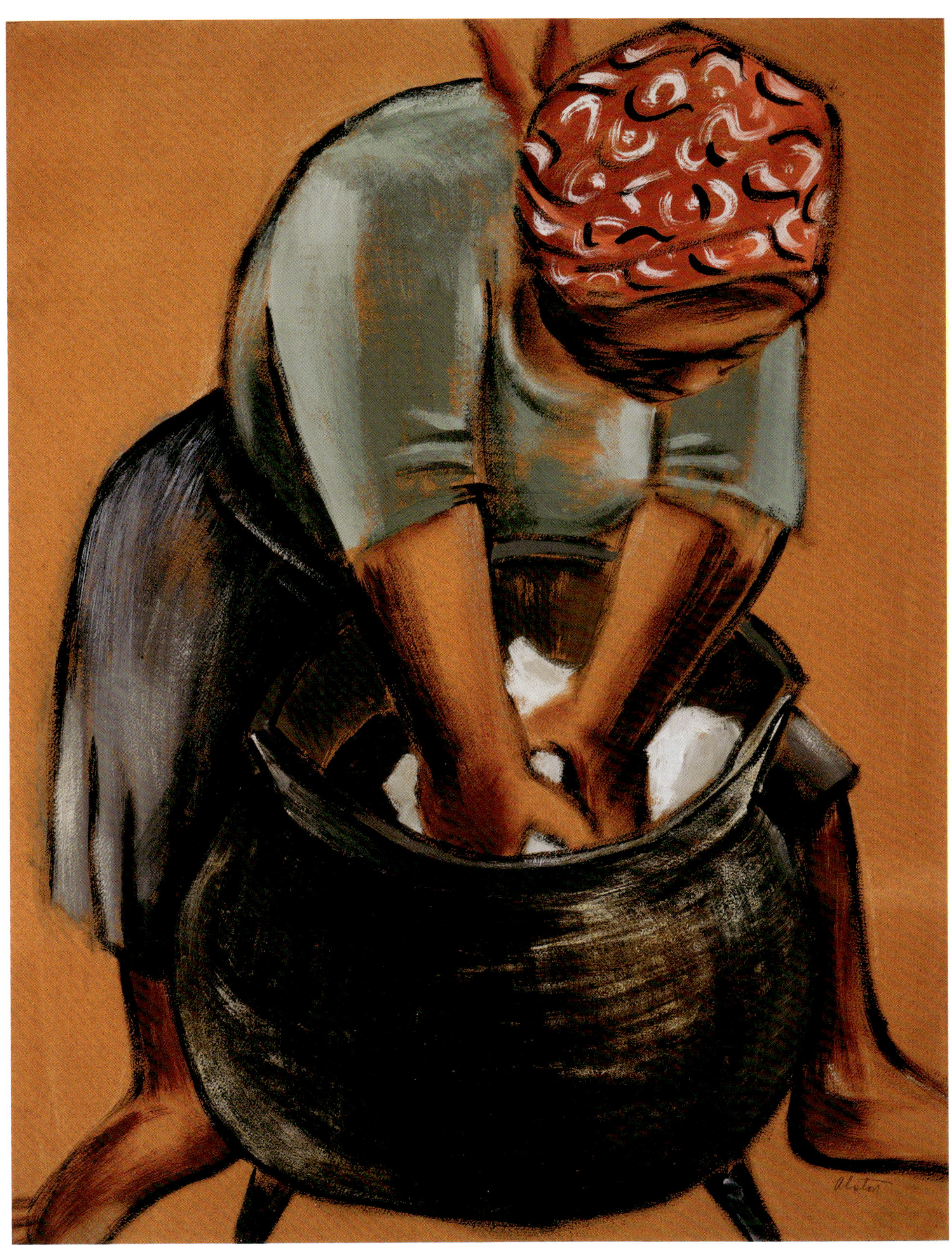

ROMARE BEARDEN

American, 1911–1988

Harlem Street Scene, c. 1973

offset lithograph on paper

30 × 24 in.

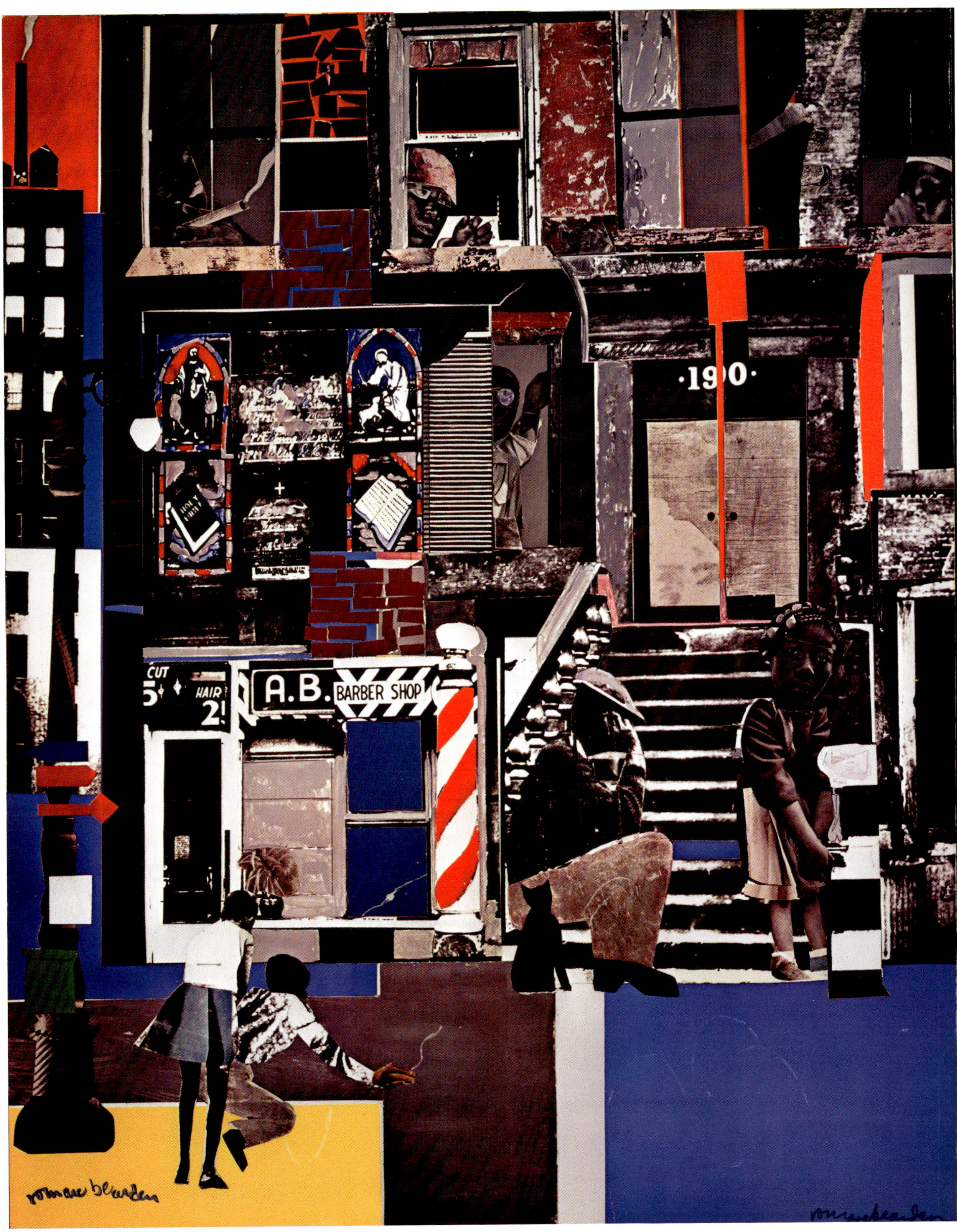
CUT
HAIR
A.B.
BARBER SHOP
·190·

ROMARE BEARDEN

American, 1911–1988

Homage to Mary Lou, 1984

lithograph on paper

29 × 20 in.

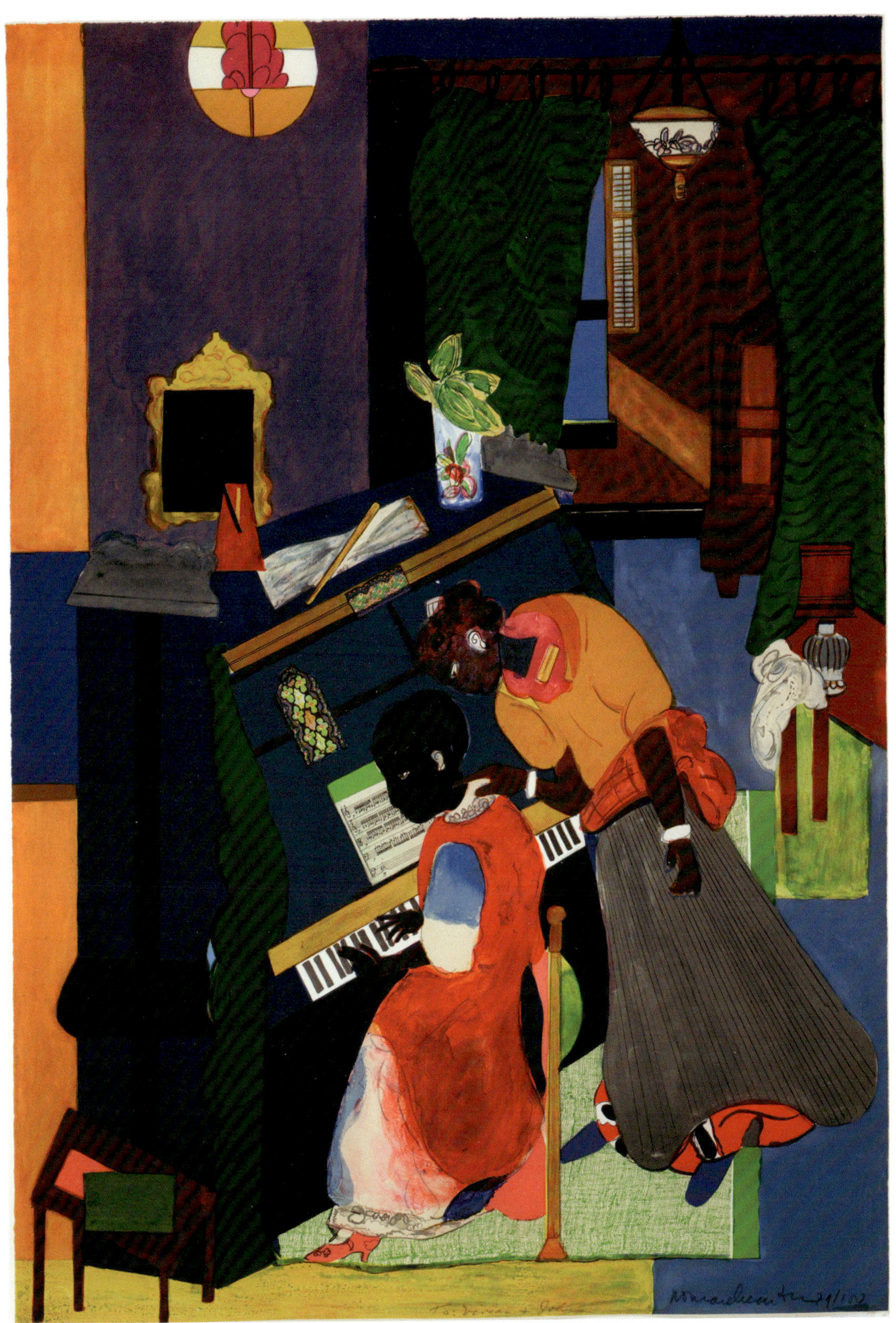

ROMARE BEARDEN

American, 1911–1988

Jamming at the Savoy, c. 1988

lithograph on paper

22 × 30 in.

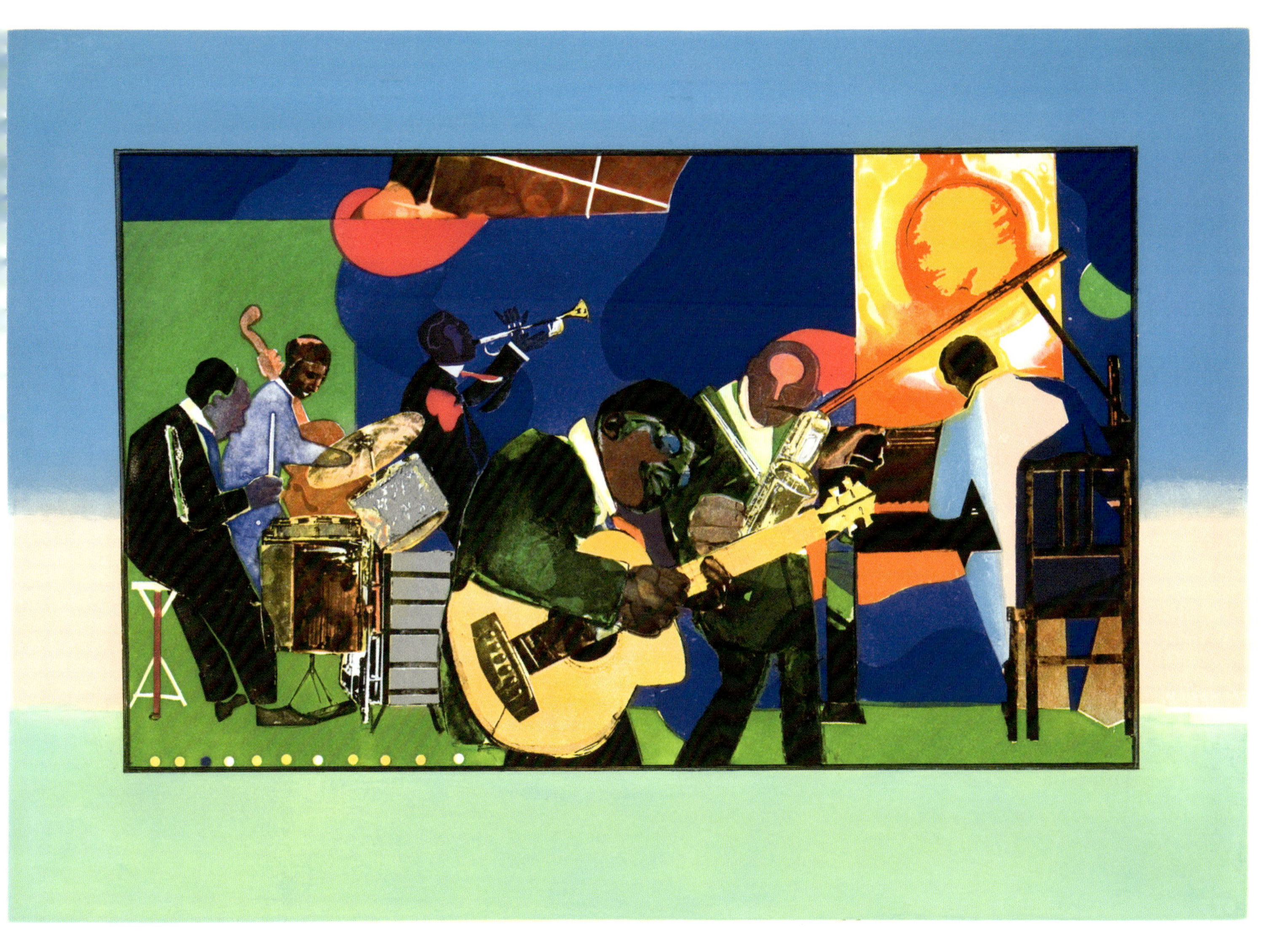

ROMARE BEARDEN
American, 1911–1988
Morning Ritual, 1986
collage and acrylic on plywood
20 × 6 ¾ in.

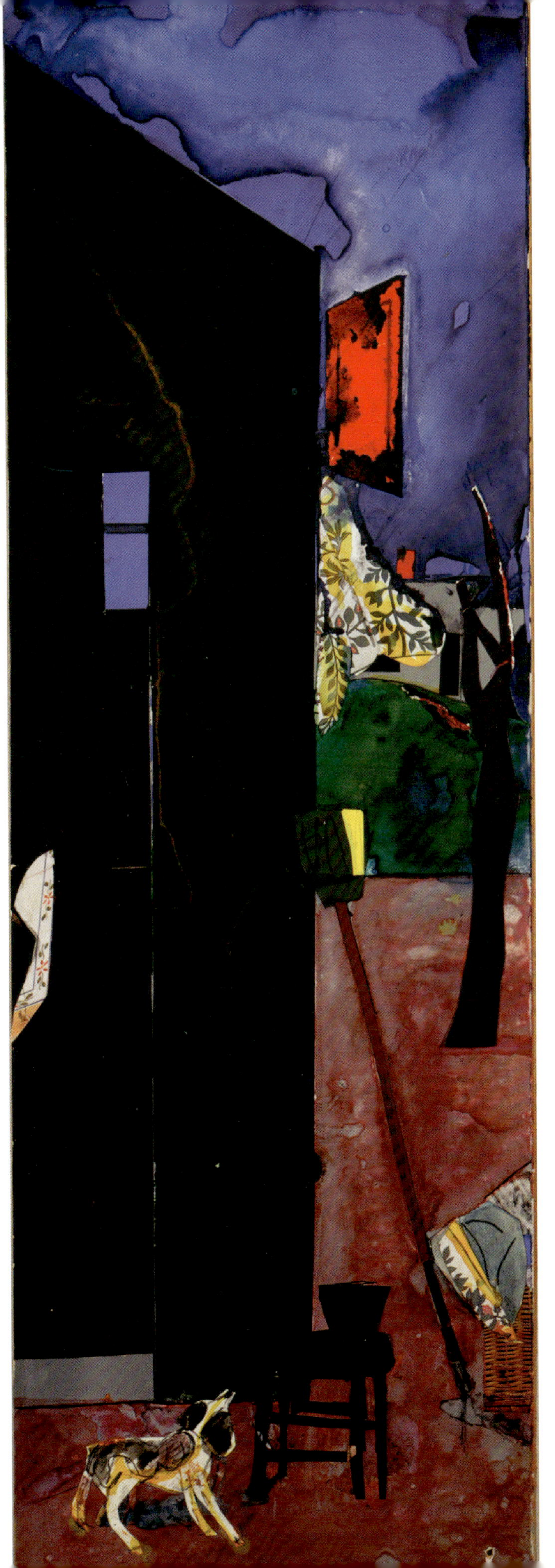

JOHN T. BIGGERS
American, 1924–2001
Family #1, 1974
charcoal on paper
32 × 23 in.

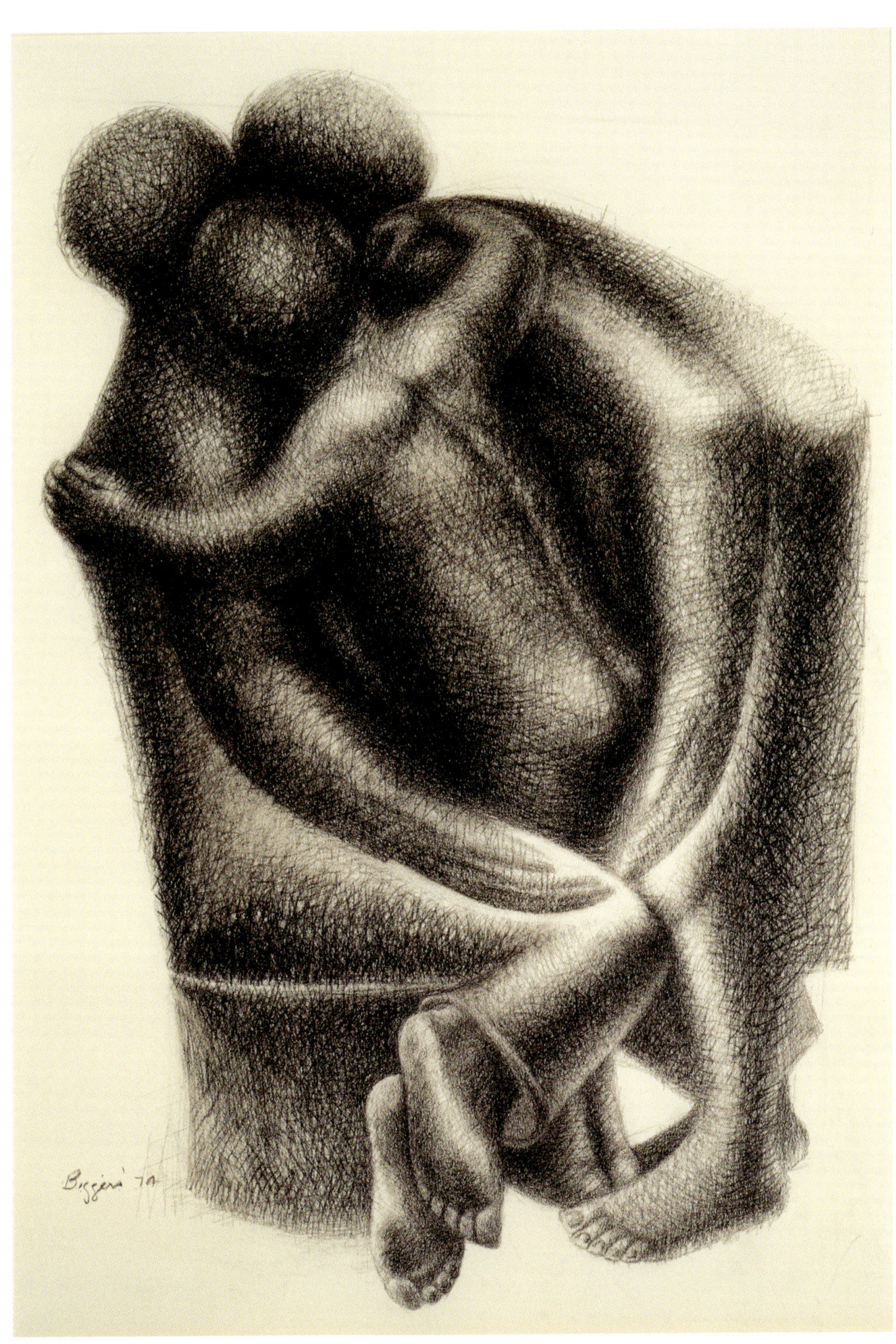

JOHN T. BIGGERS

American, 1924–2001

Family #2, 1975

lithograph on paper

26 × 20 in.

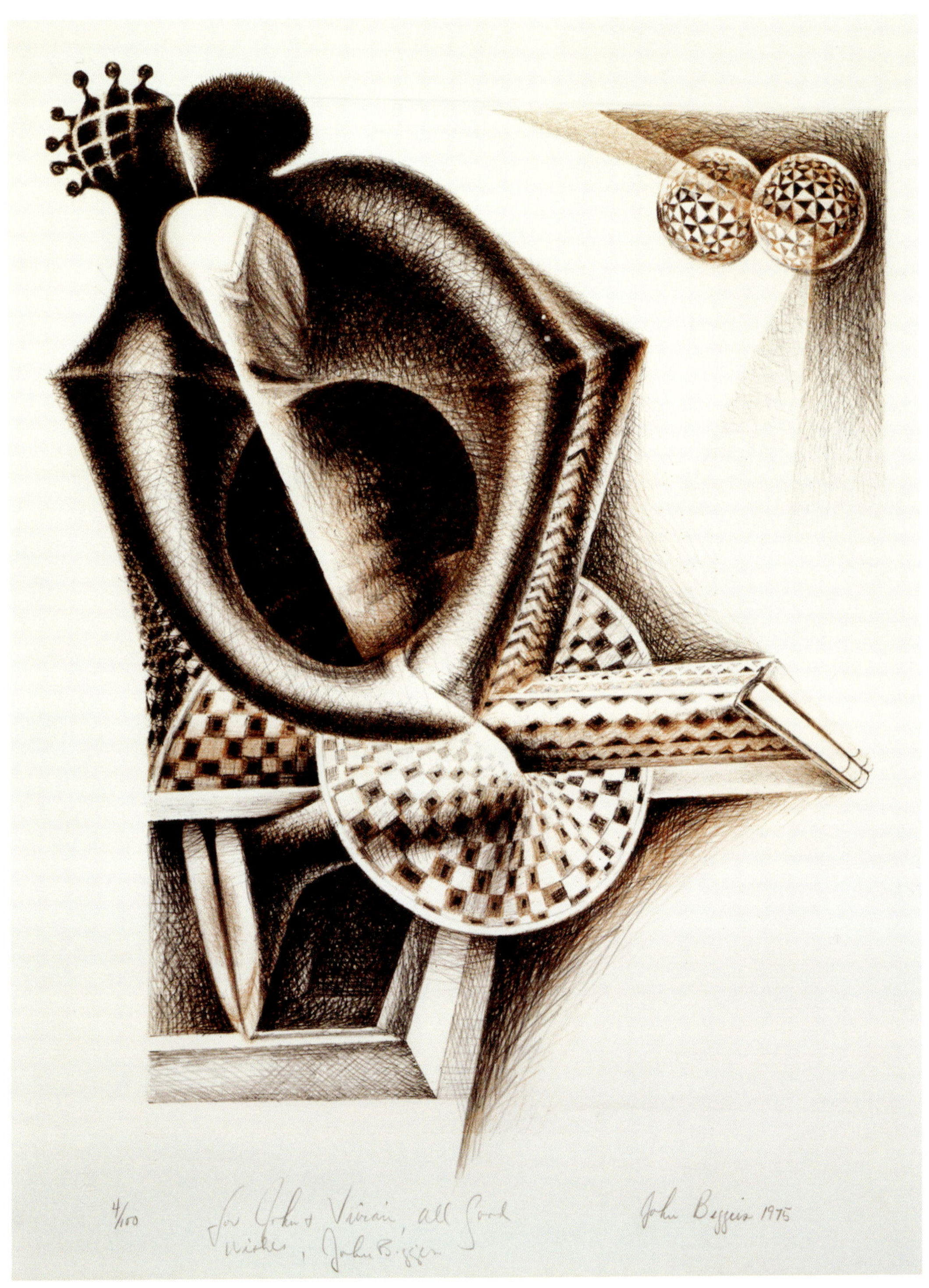
4/100
for John + Vivian, all Good Wishes, John Biggers
John Biggers 1975

JOHN T. BIGGERS

American, 1924–2001

Twins of Morning, 1975

lithograph on paper

26 × 20 in.

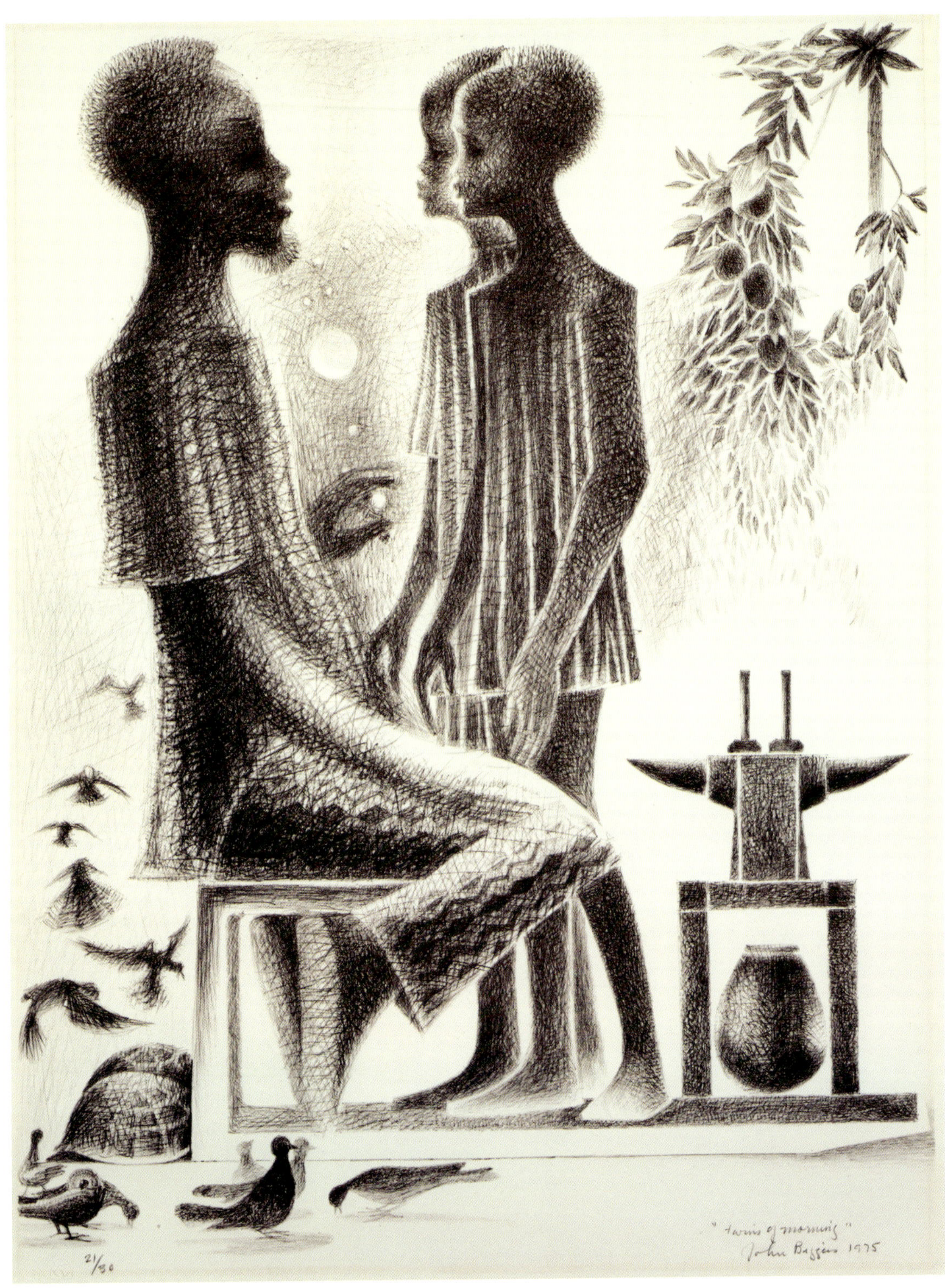
"twins of morning"
John Biggers 1975
21/30

MARGARET BURROUGHS
American, 1917–2010
Warsaw, 1965
linocut on paper
17 × 13 ¾ in.

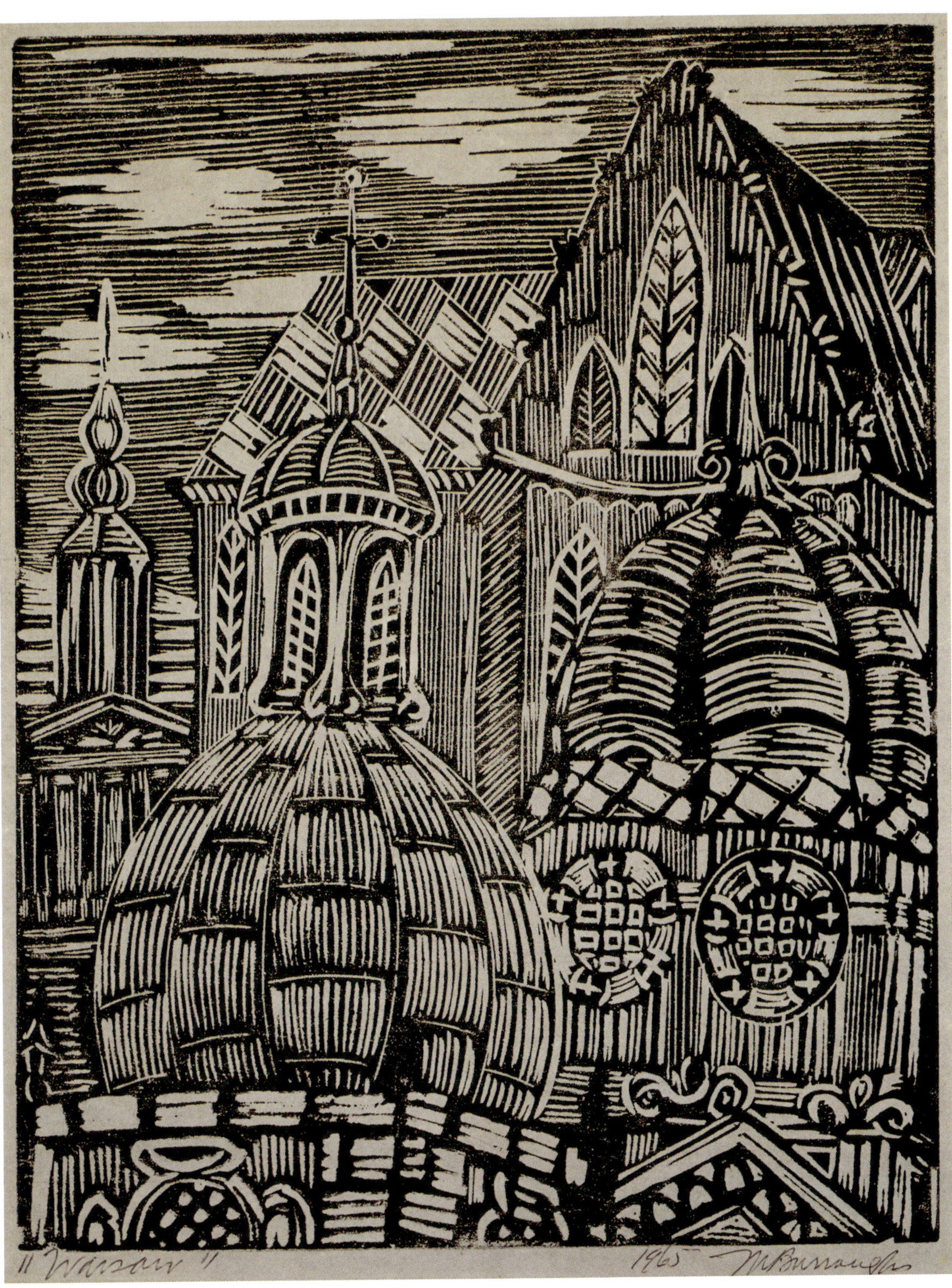
"Warsaw"
1965

ELIZABETH CATLETT
American, 1915–2012; active Mexico, 1947–2012
Head of a Woman, 1967
lithograph on paper
19 3/8 × 14 ½ in.

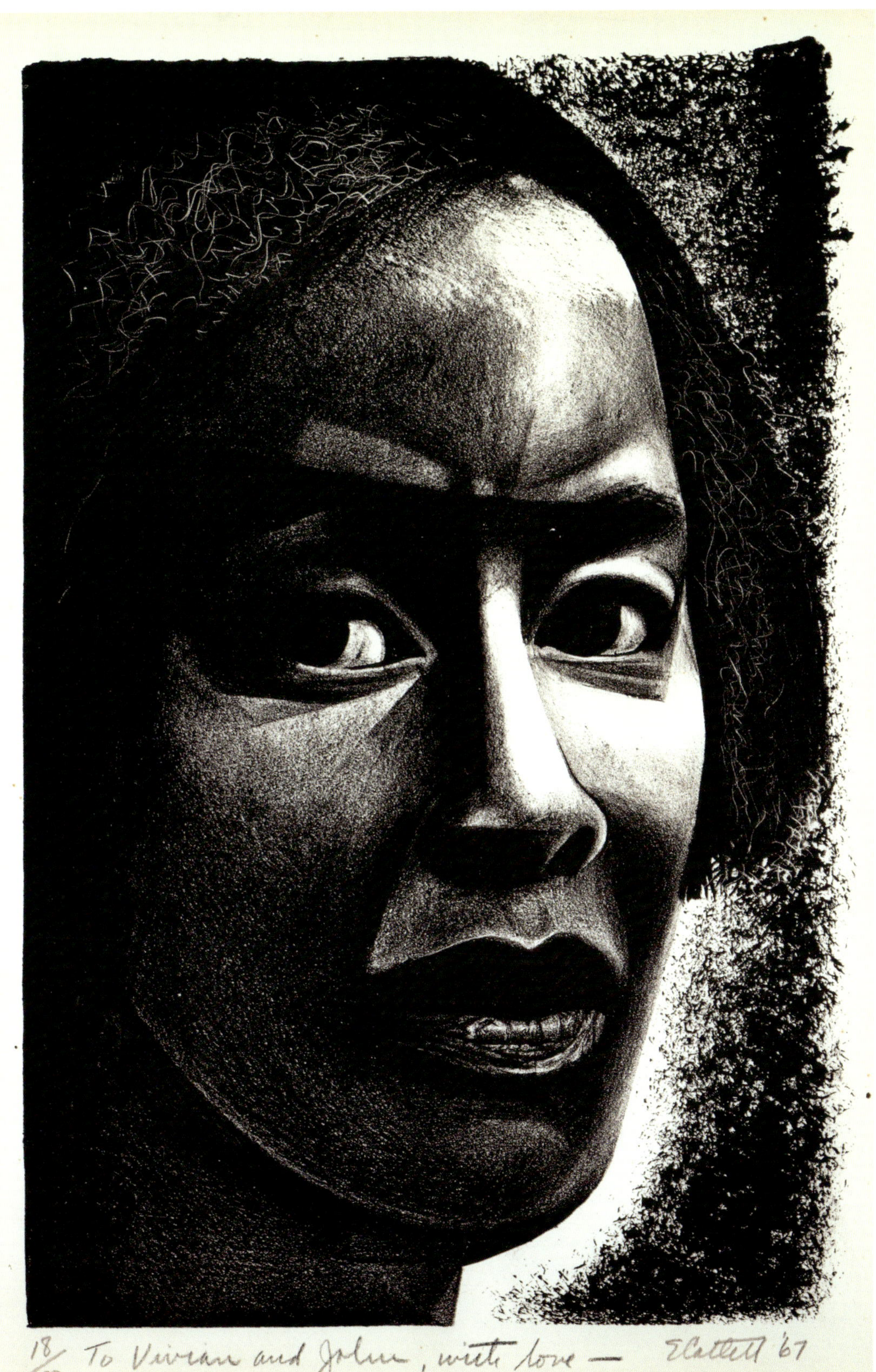
18/50
To Vivian and John, with love —
ECatlett '67

ERNEST CRICHLOW
American, 1914–2005
Boy in a Green Field, c. 1979
acrylic on composition board
31 × 21 in.

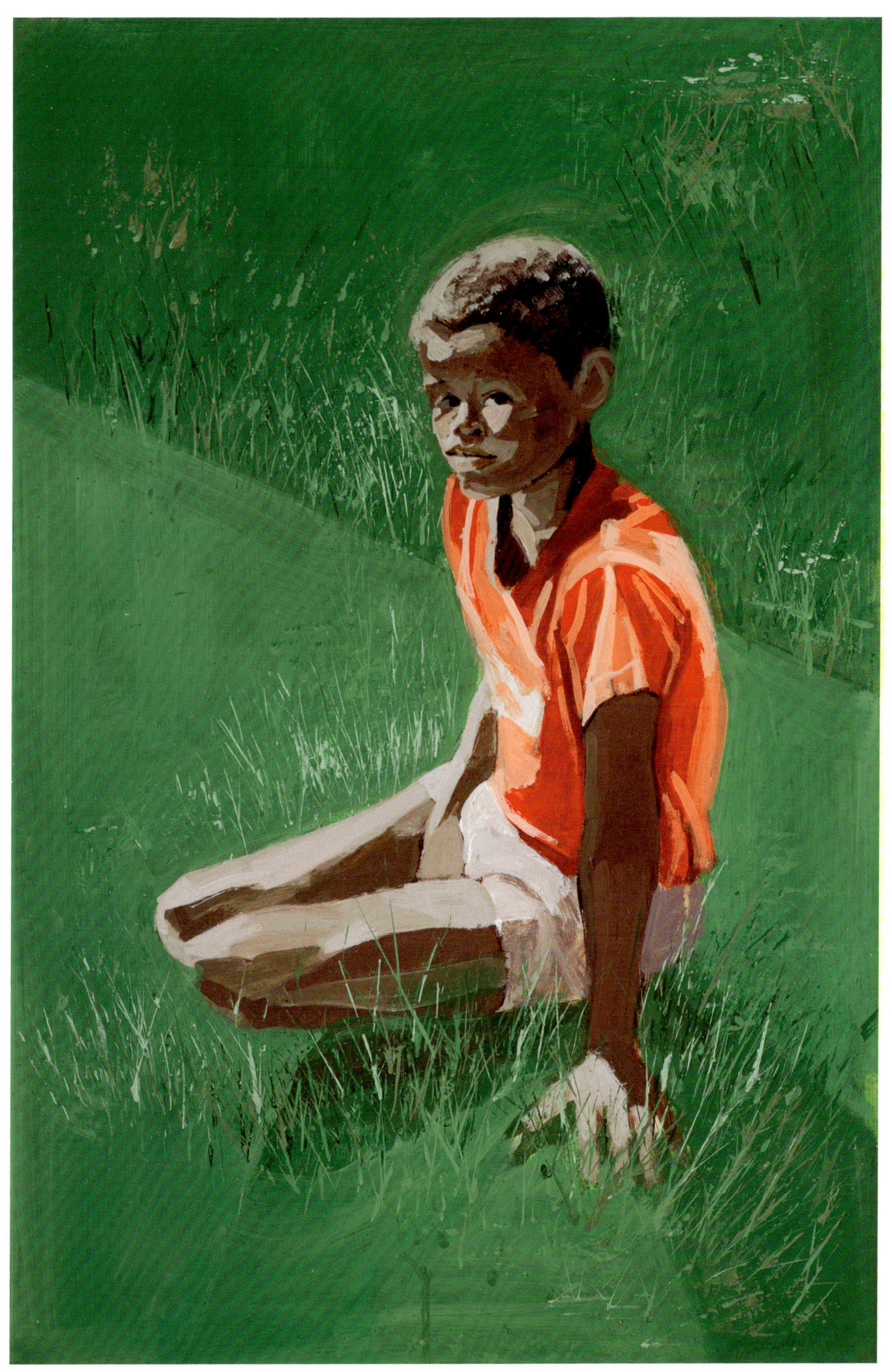

ERNEST CRICHLOW

American, 1914–2005

The Balcony, 1980

collage and acrylic on paper

15 × 20 in.

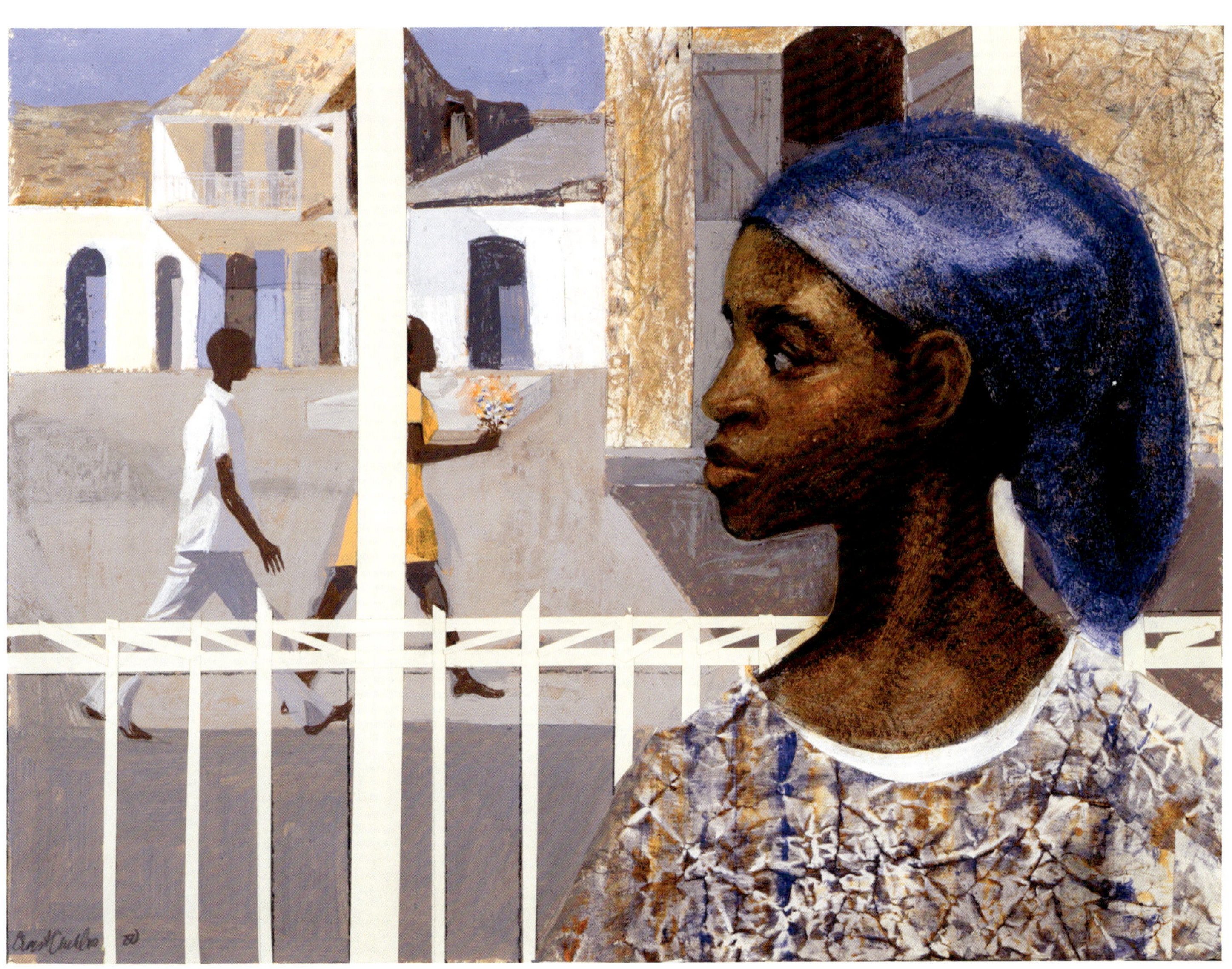

ERNEST CRICHLOW
American, 1914–2005
Girl with Flowers, c. 1979
acrylic on composition board
31 × 21 in.

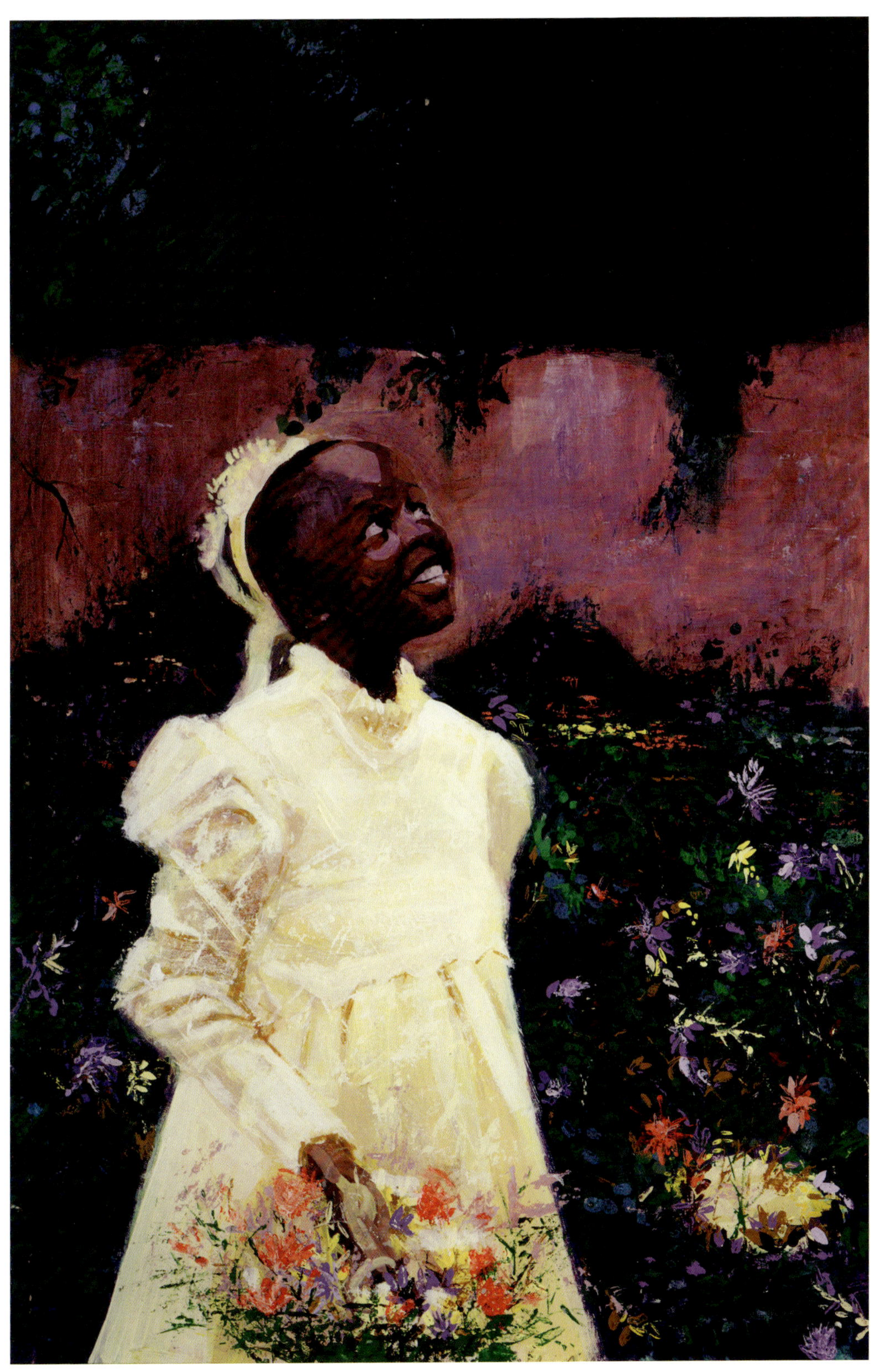

ERNEST CRICHLOW

American, 1914–2005

Ronnie, 1965

lithograph on paper

20 × 13 in.

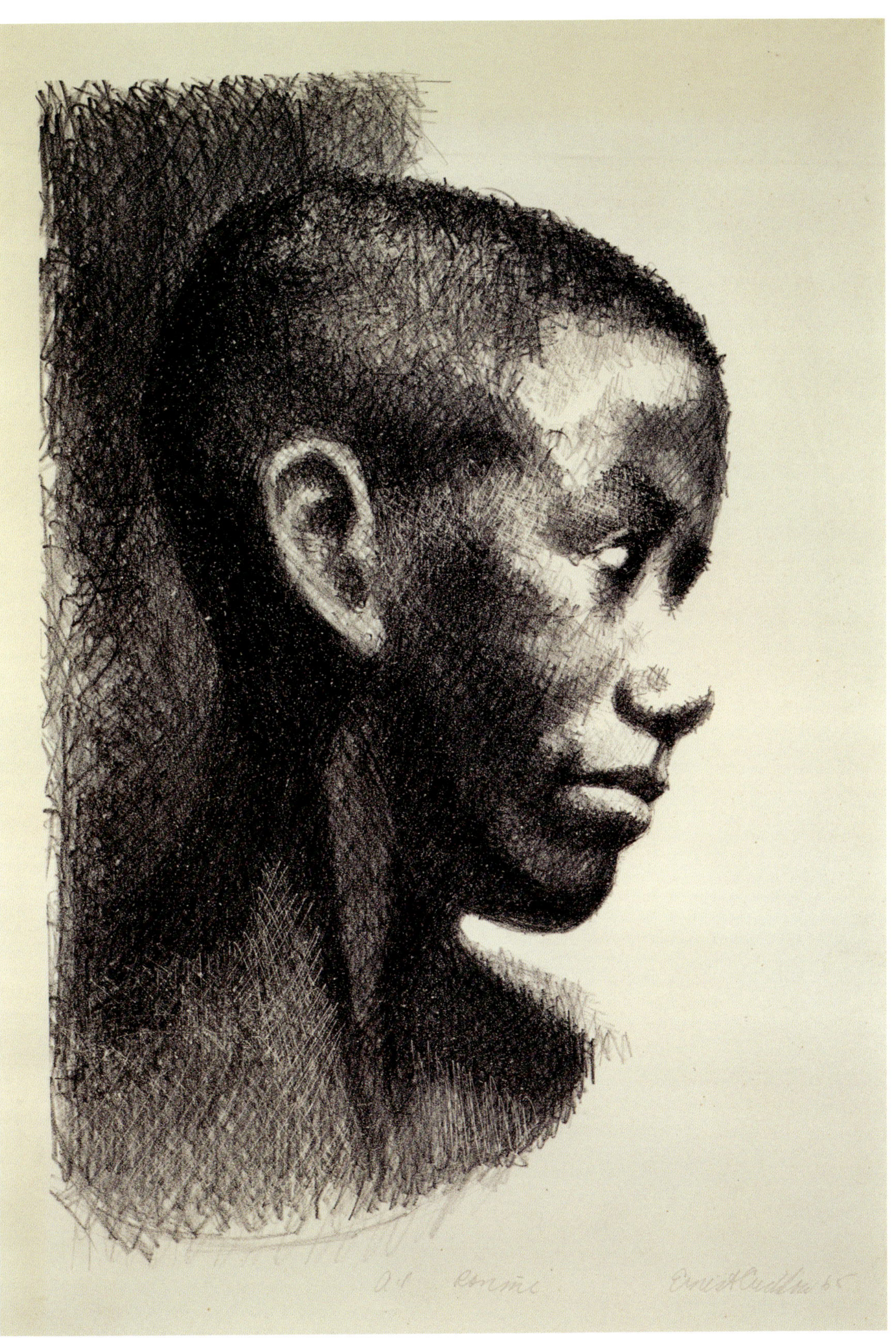

ERNEST CRICHLOW
American, 1914–2005
Street Princess, 1982
serigraph on paper
38 5/8 × 26 ¼ in.

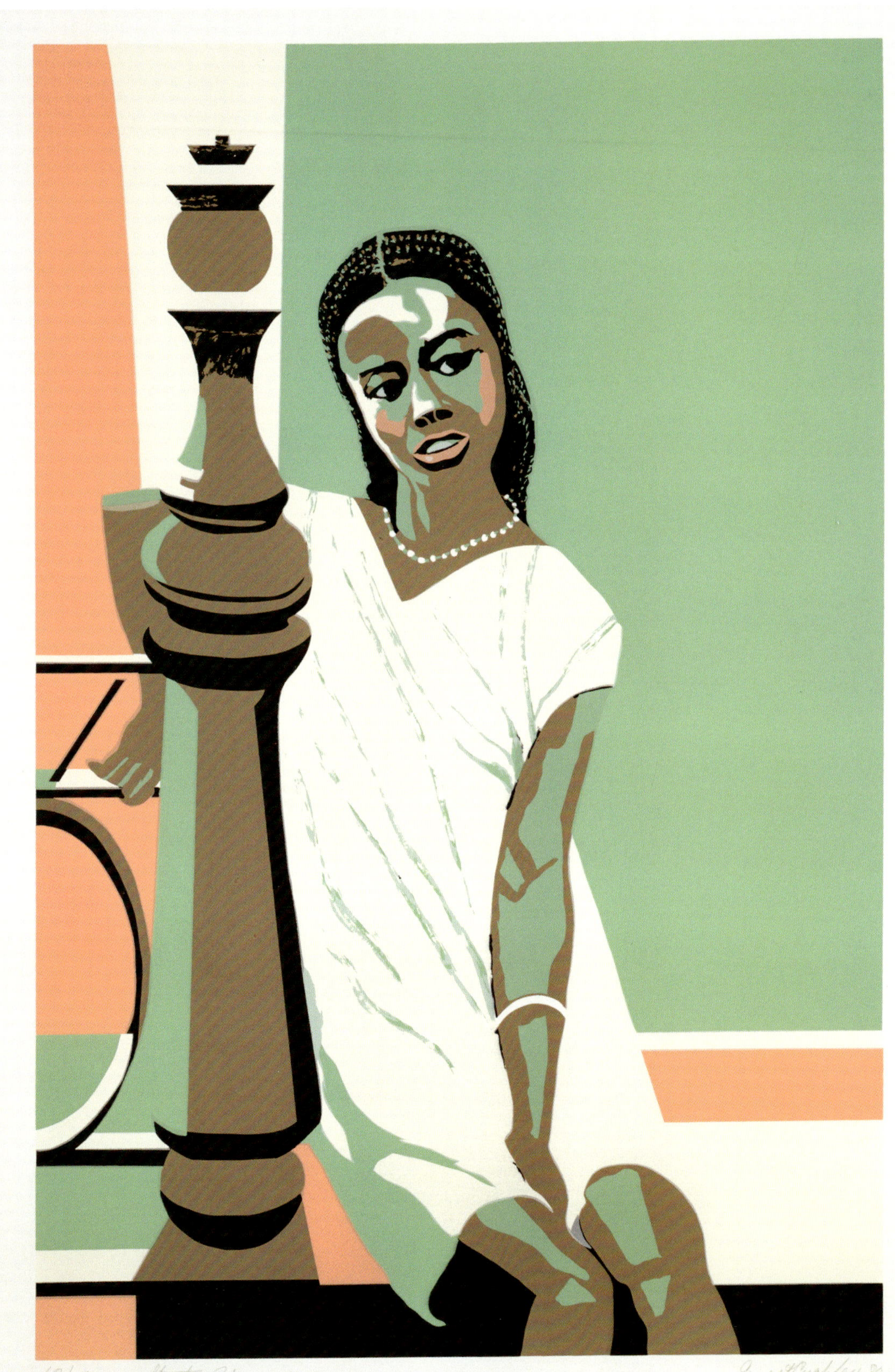
63/100

ERNEST CRICHLOW

American, 1914–2005

The Sisters, 1979

serigraph on paper

26 ¼ × 40 in.

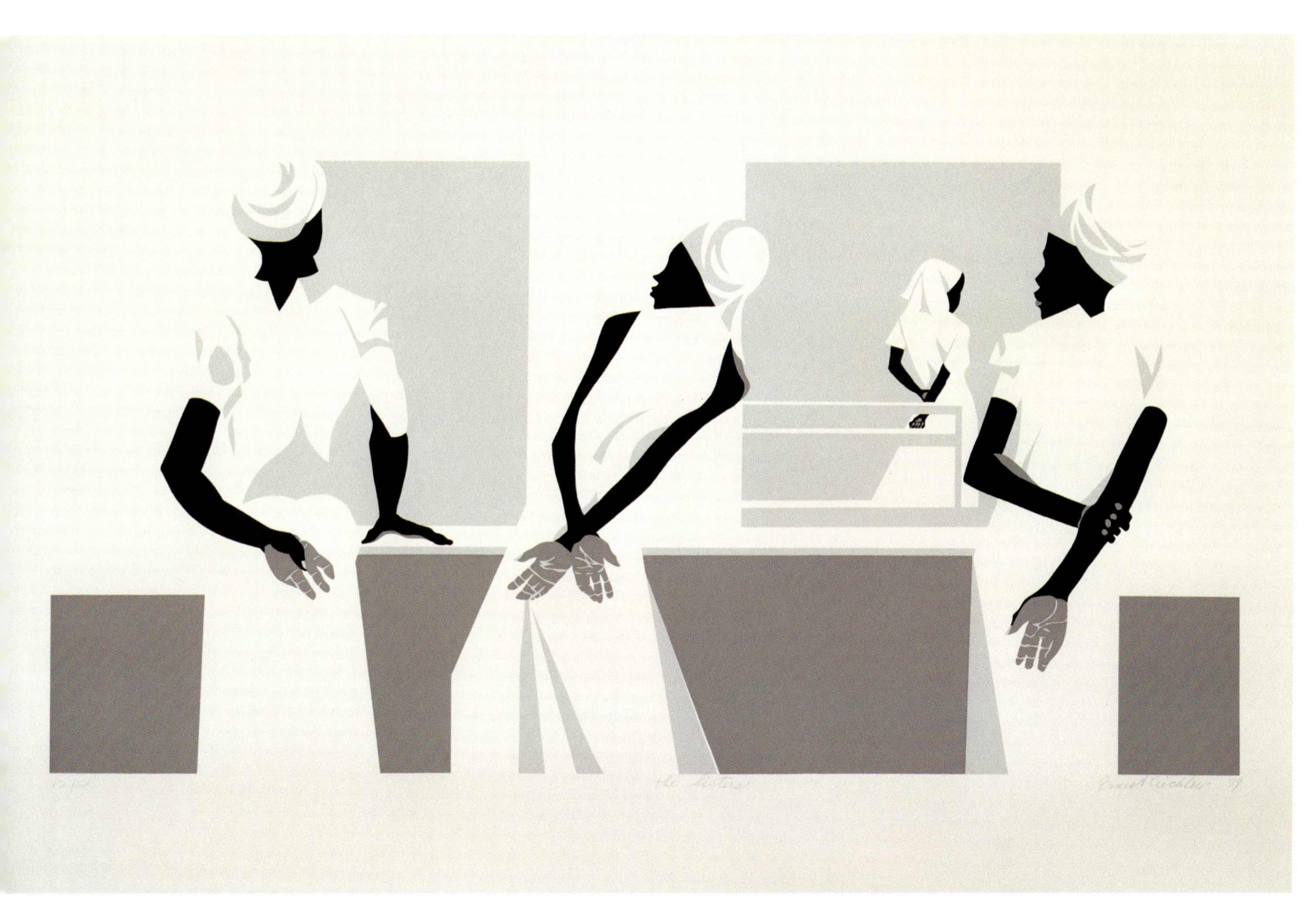

ERNEST CRICHLOW

American, 1914–2005

Suburban Woman, 1979

intaglio print with applied gouache, acrylic and collage

19 ¾ × 15 in.

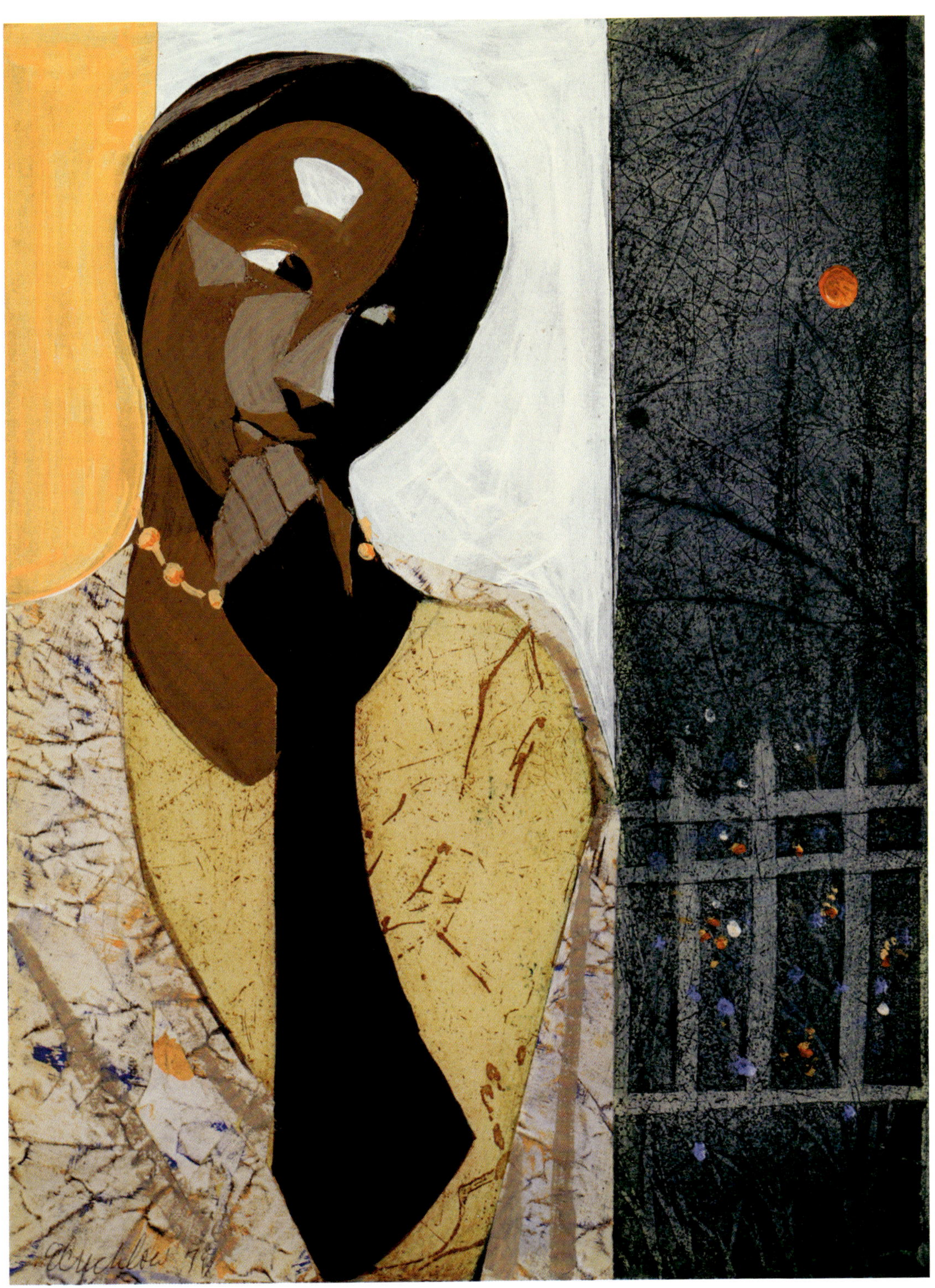

ERNEST CRICHLOW
American, 1914–2005
Waiting, c. 1965
lithograph on paper
19 ½ × 14 in.

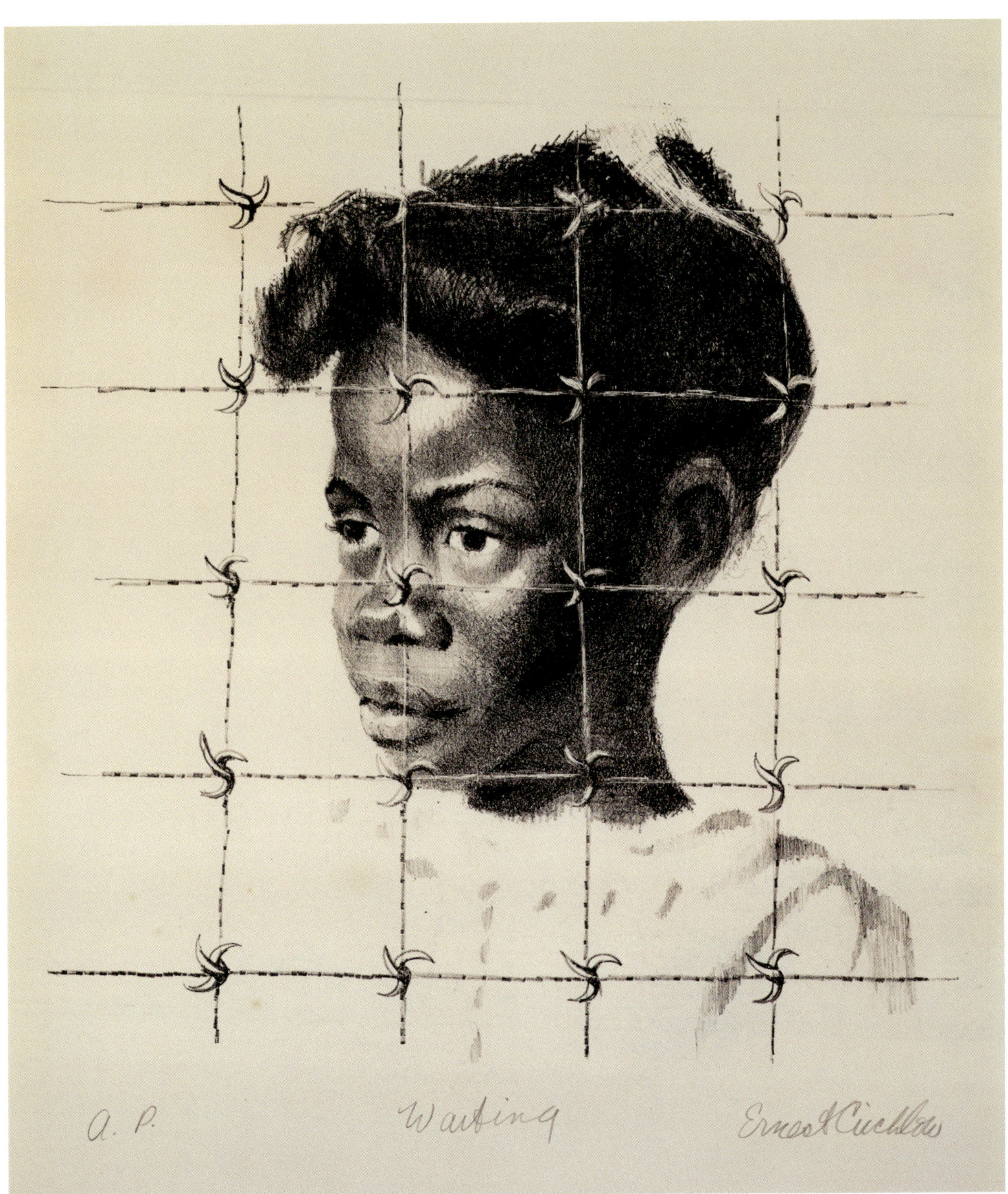
A. P.
Waiting
Ernest Crichlow

ERNEST CRICHLOW

American, 1914–2005

Woman in a Blue Coat, c. 1948

oil on canvas

20 × 16 in.

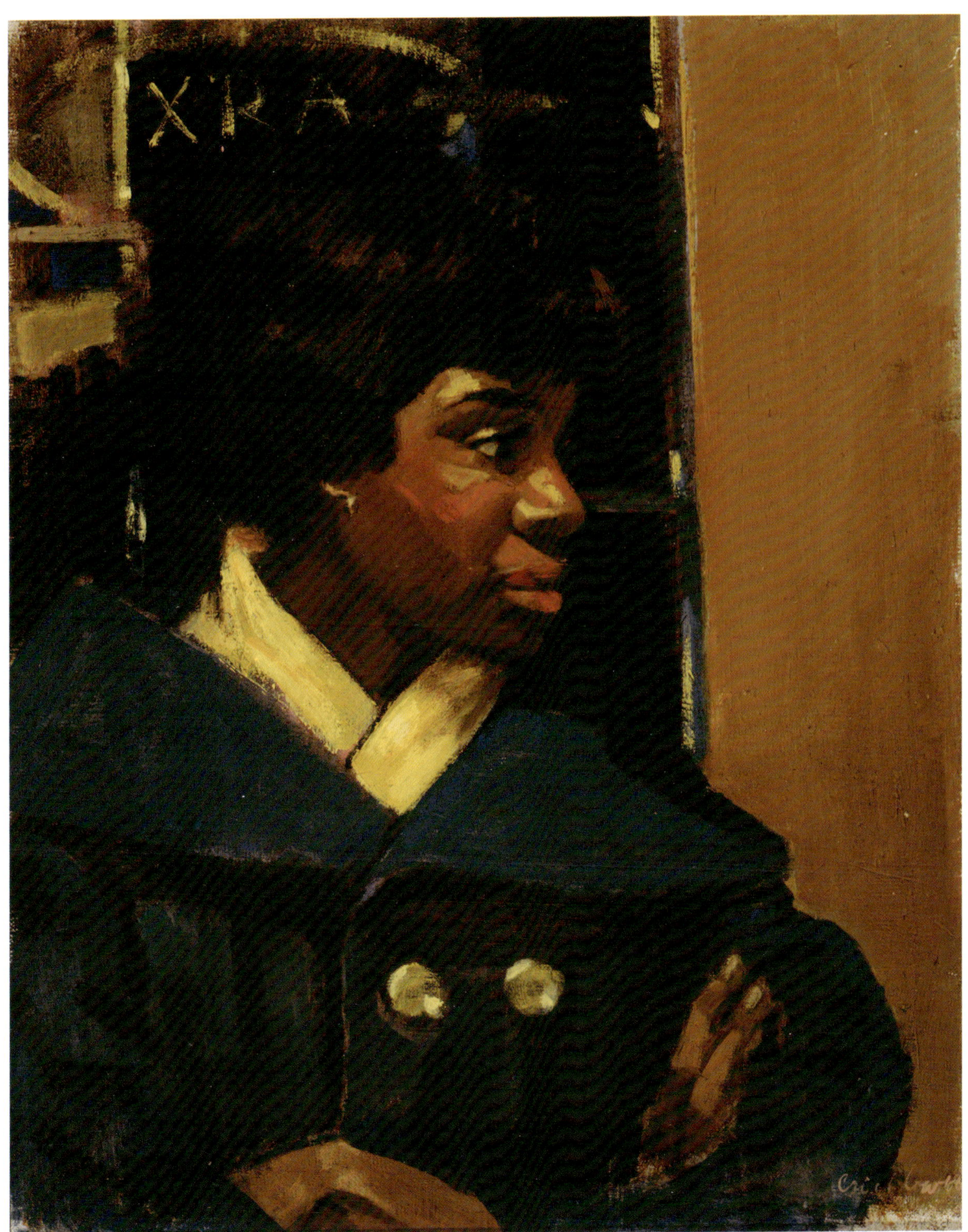
XRA

ERNEST CRICHLOW

American, 1914–2005
Woman in Yellow Dress, c. 1980
intaglio print with applied collage and tempera paint
22 × 17 in.

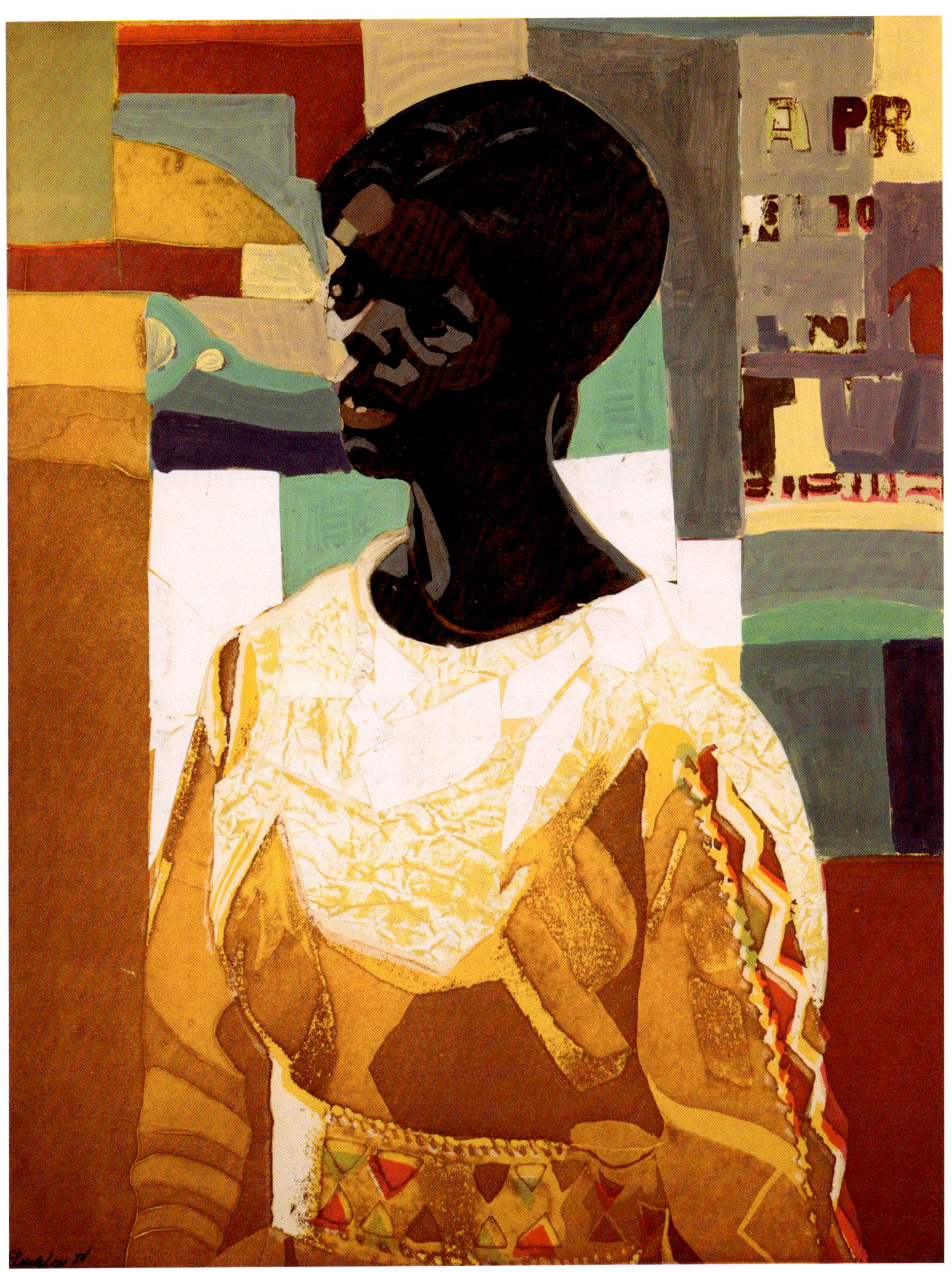
A PR

JAMES DENMARK

American, b. 1936

Daily Gossip, c. 1975

collage on panel

8 ½ × 7 in.

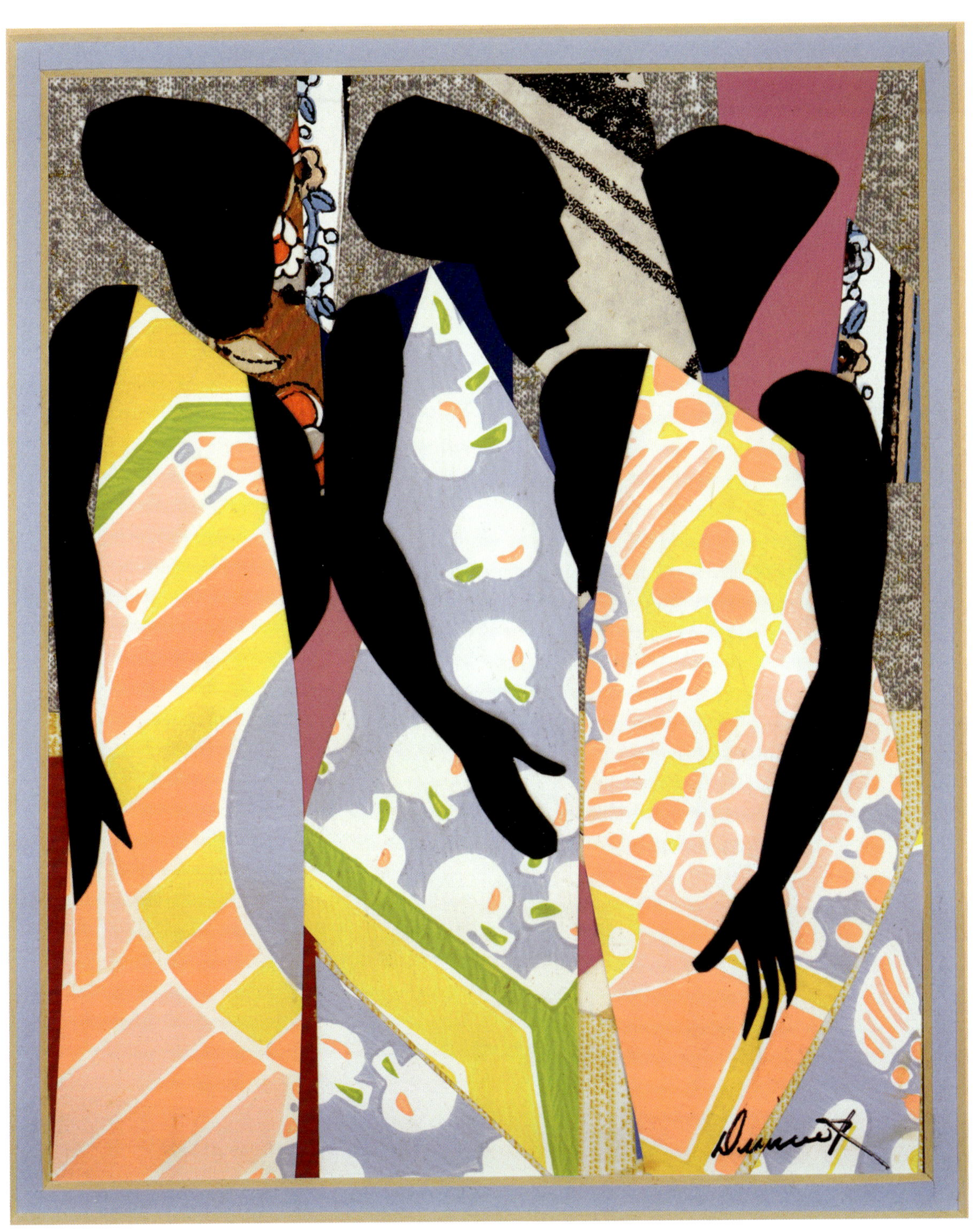

JAMES DENMARK

American, b. 1936

Head, 1973

collage on panel

20 × 14 ¼ in.

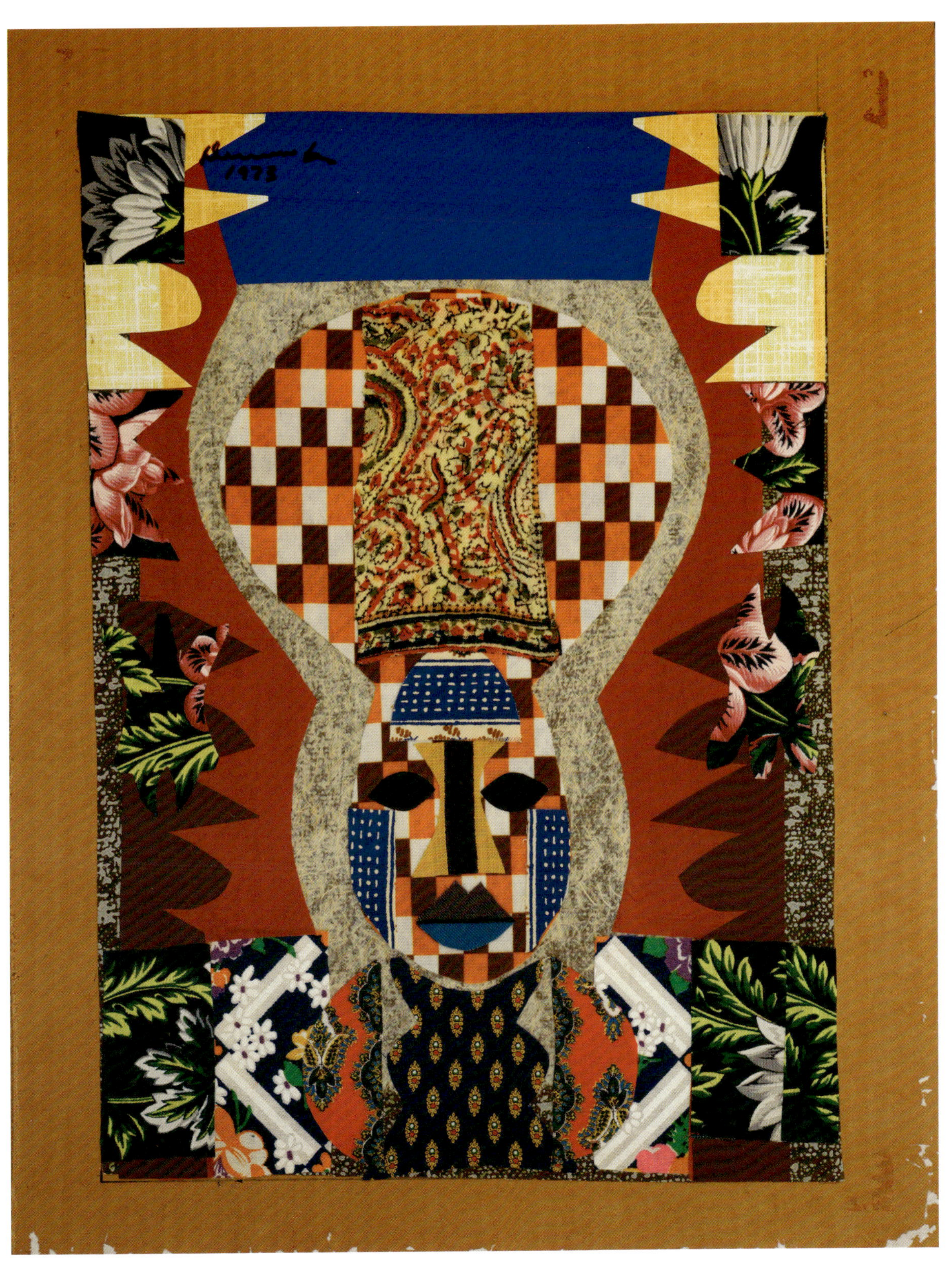

JAMES DENMARK

American, b. 1936

Two Generations, 1984

offset lithograph on paper

28 × 22 in.

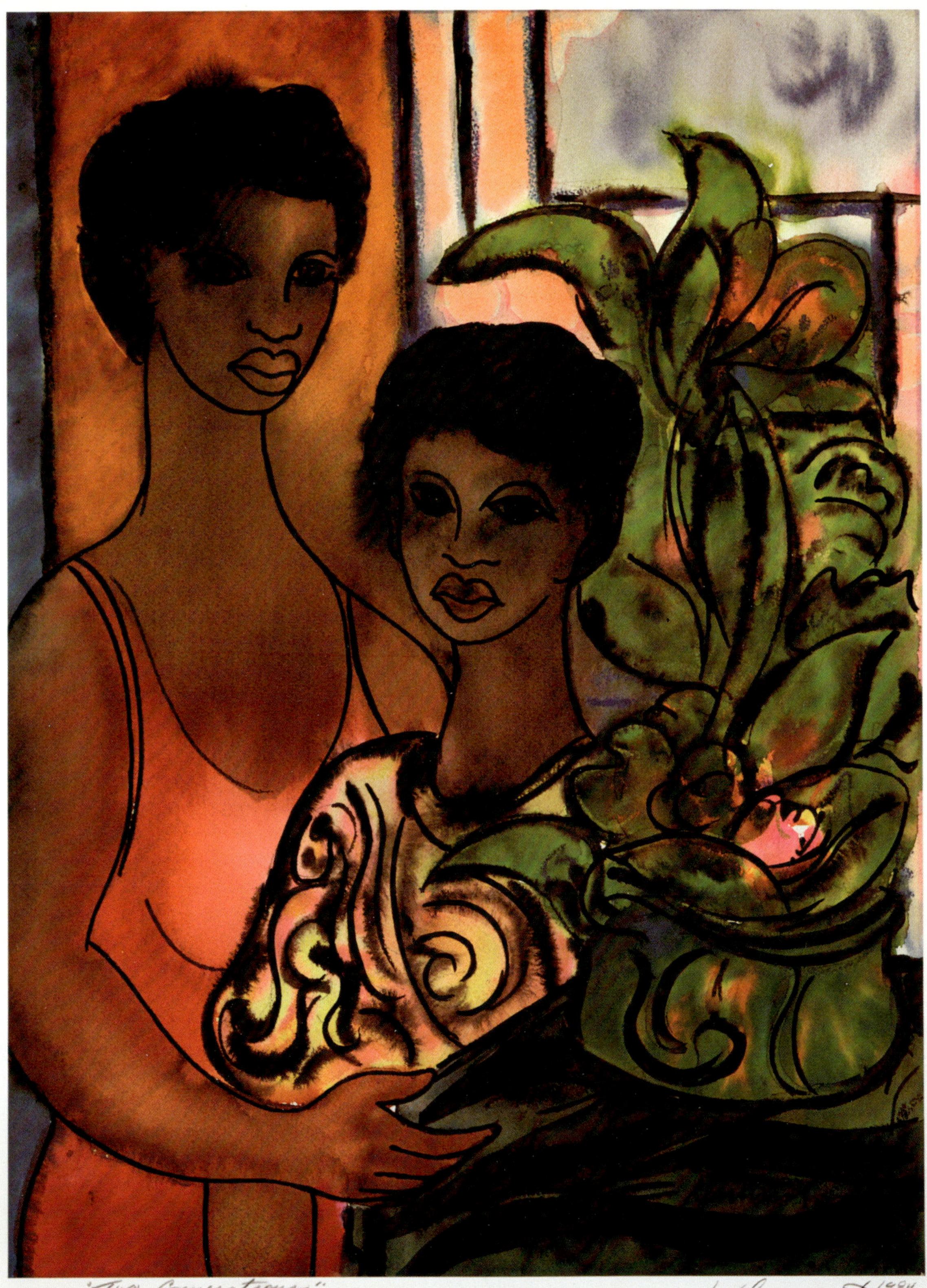
"Two Generations"
1984

JAMES DENMARK

American, b. 1936

Untitled, c. 1983

watercolor and crayon on paper

14 × 10 in.

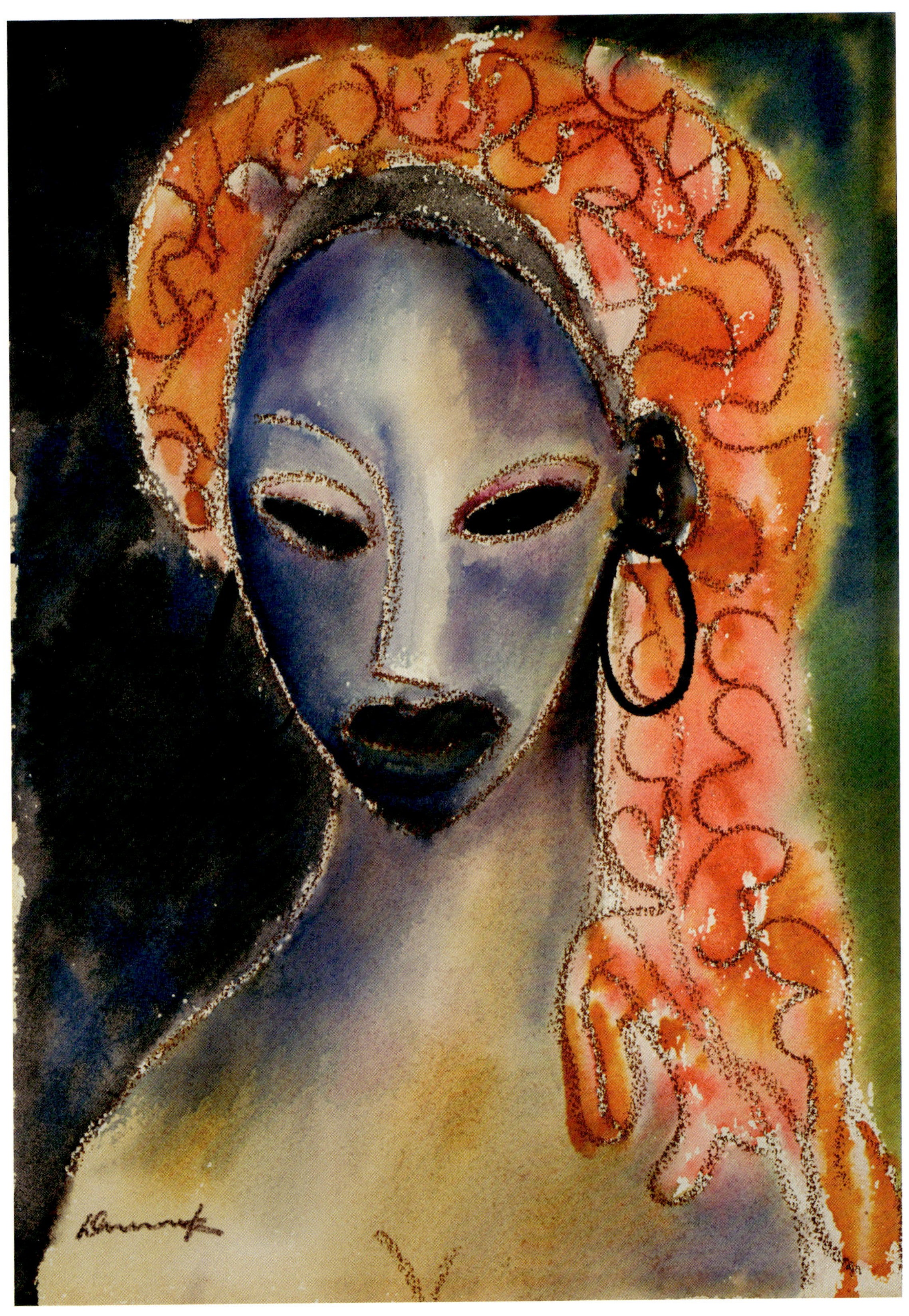

JONATHAN GREEN
American, b. 1955
Easter, 1989
acrylic on paper
11 ¼ × 7 ½ in.

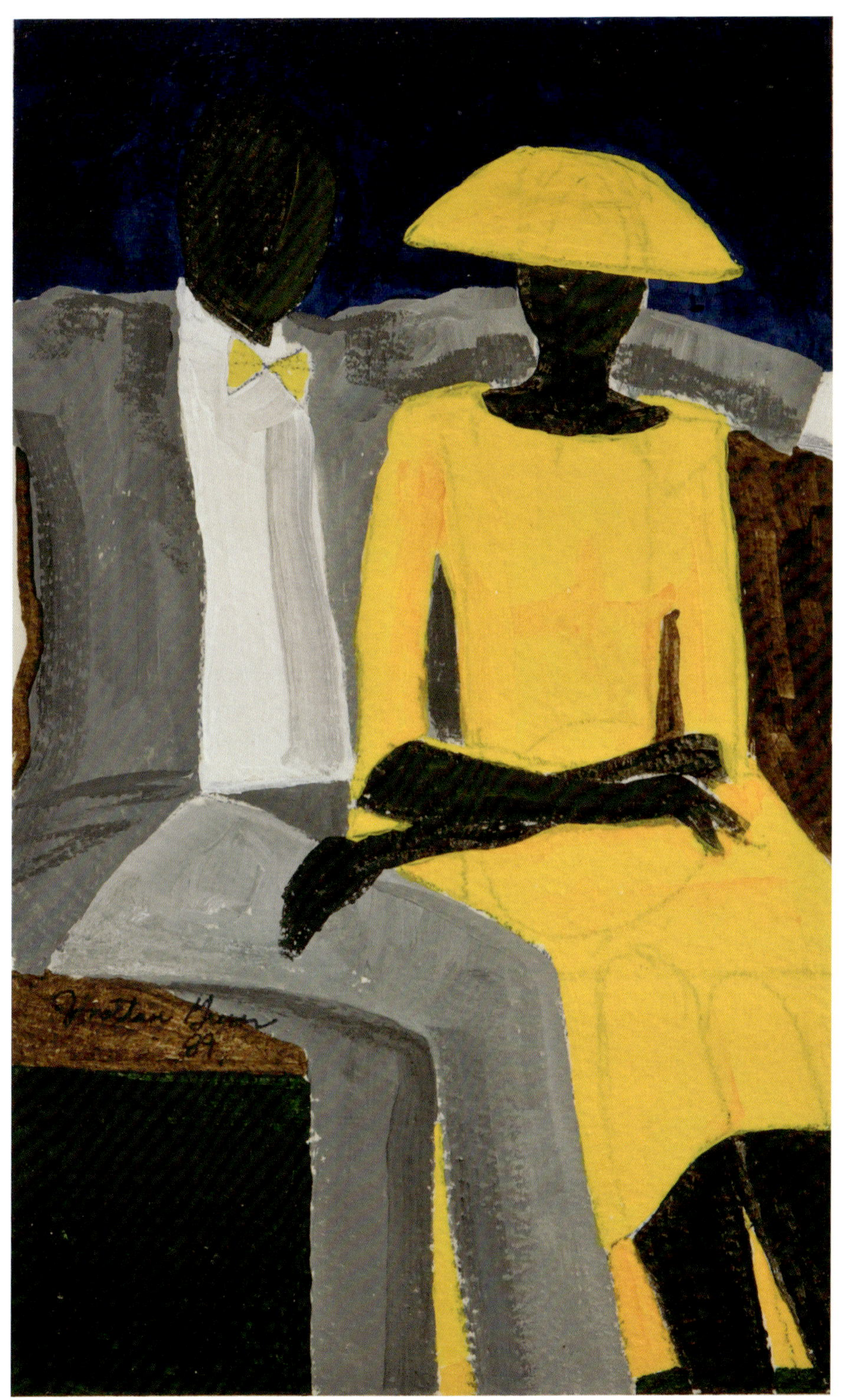

JONATHAN GREEN

American, b. 1955

Folding Sheets, 1989

acrylic on canvas

20 × 15 ¾ in.

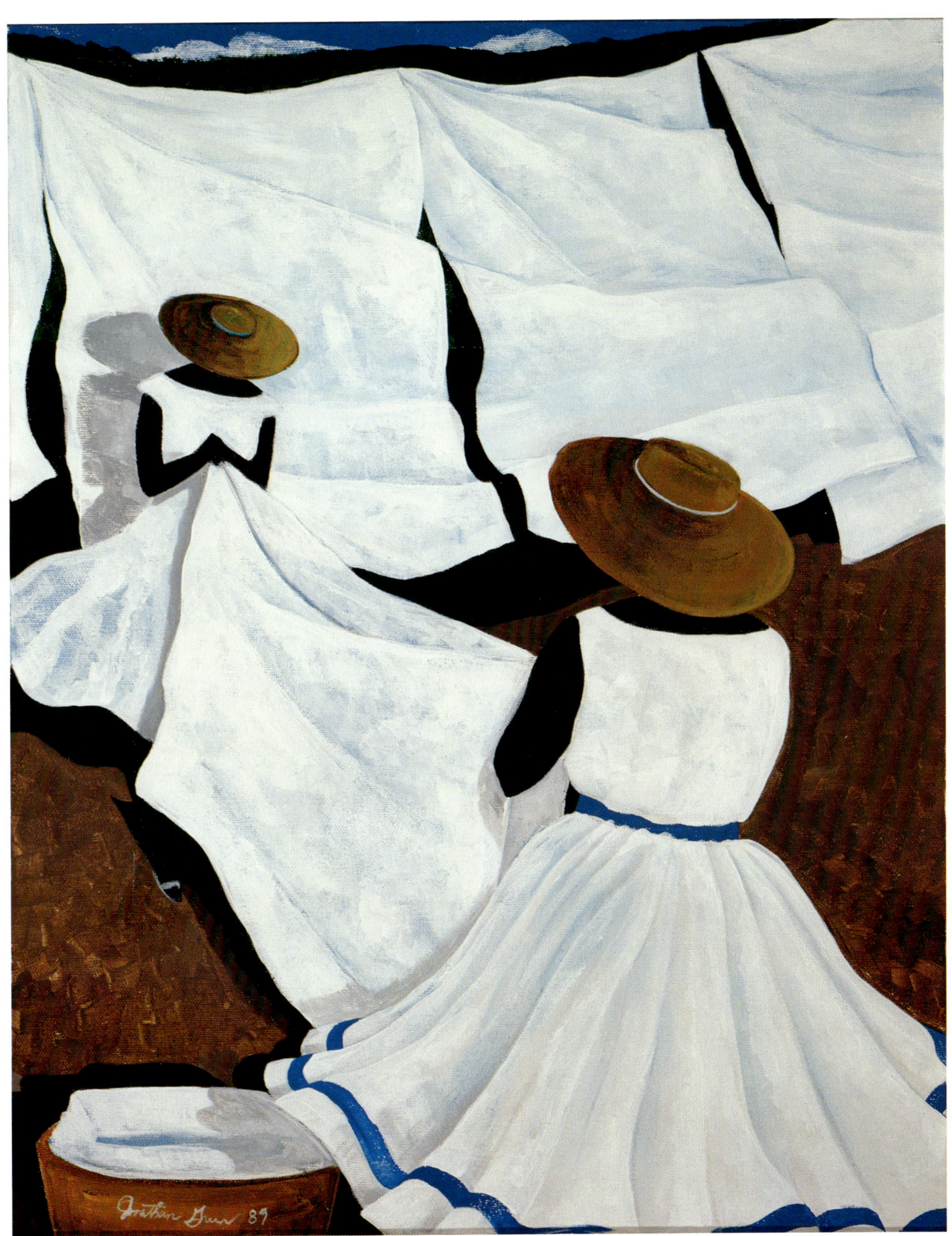

J. EUGENE GRIGSBY

American, 1918–2013

Abstraction in Red and Black, c. 1963

oil on canvas

26 × 34 in.

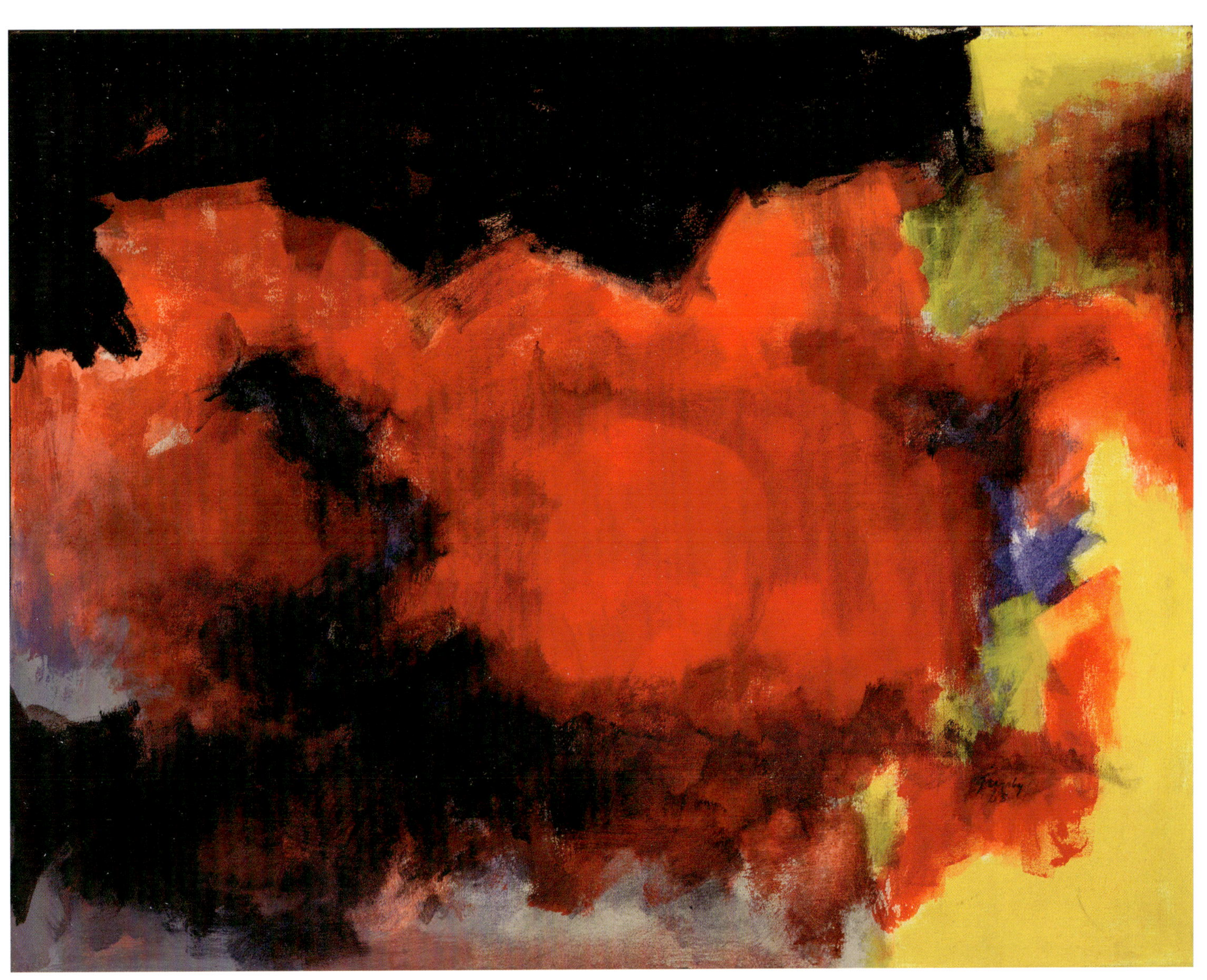

J. EUGENE GRIGSBY

American, 1918–2013

African Journey—The Bridge, c. 1981

serigraph on paper

22 × 30 in.

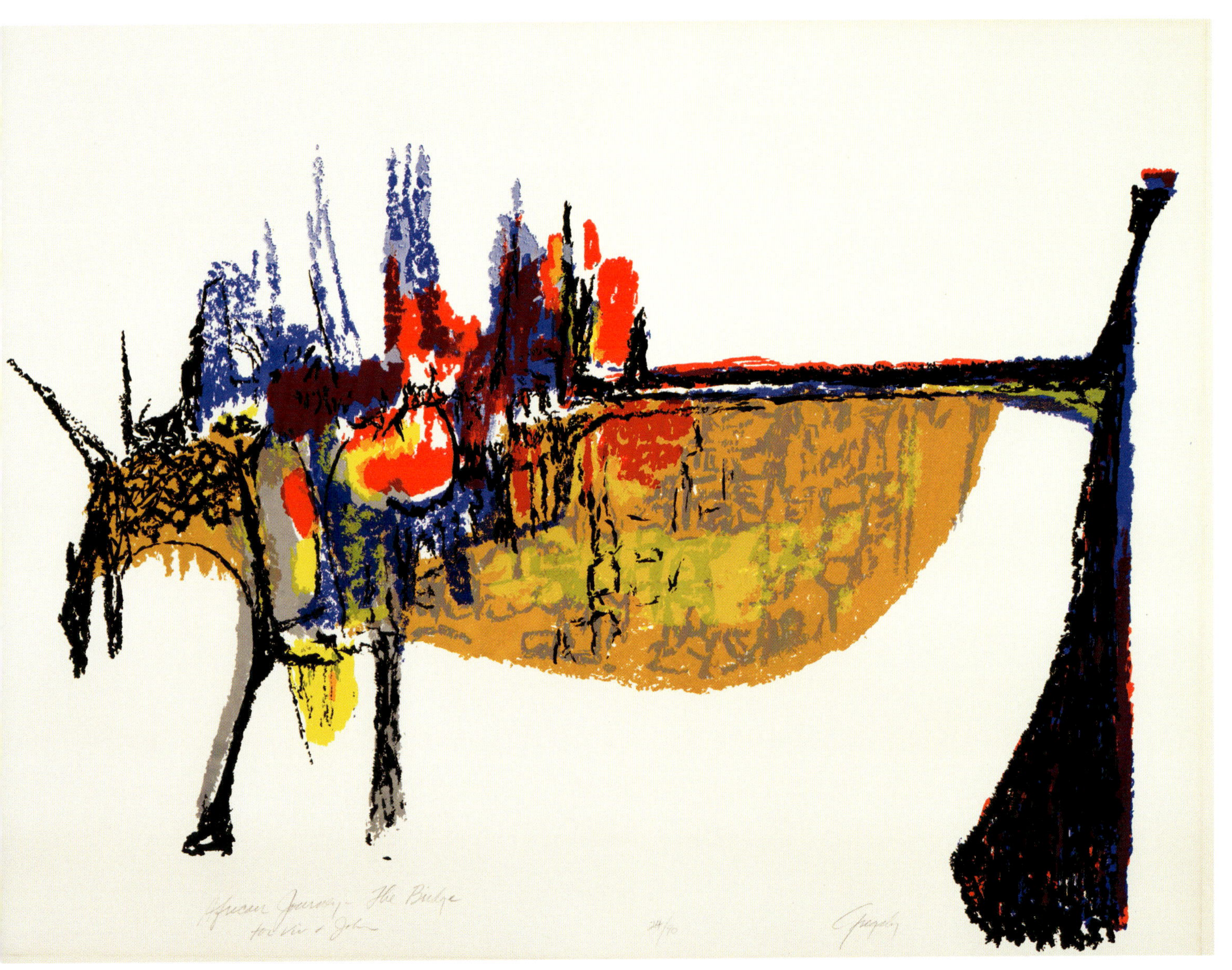

J. EUGENE GRIGSBY

American, 1918–2013

Black, Brown and Beige, 1963

oil on canvas

20 × 30 ½ in.

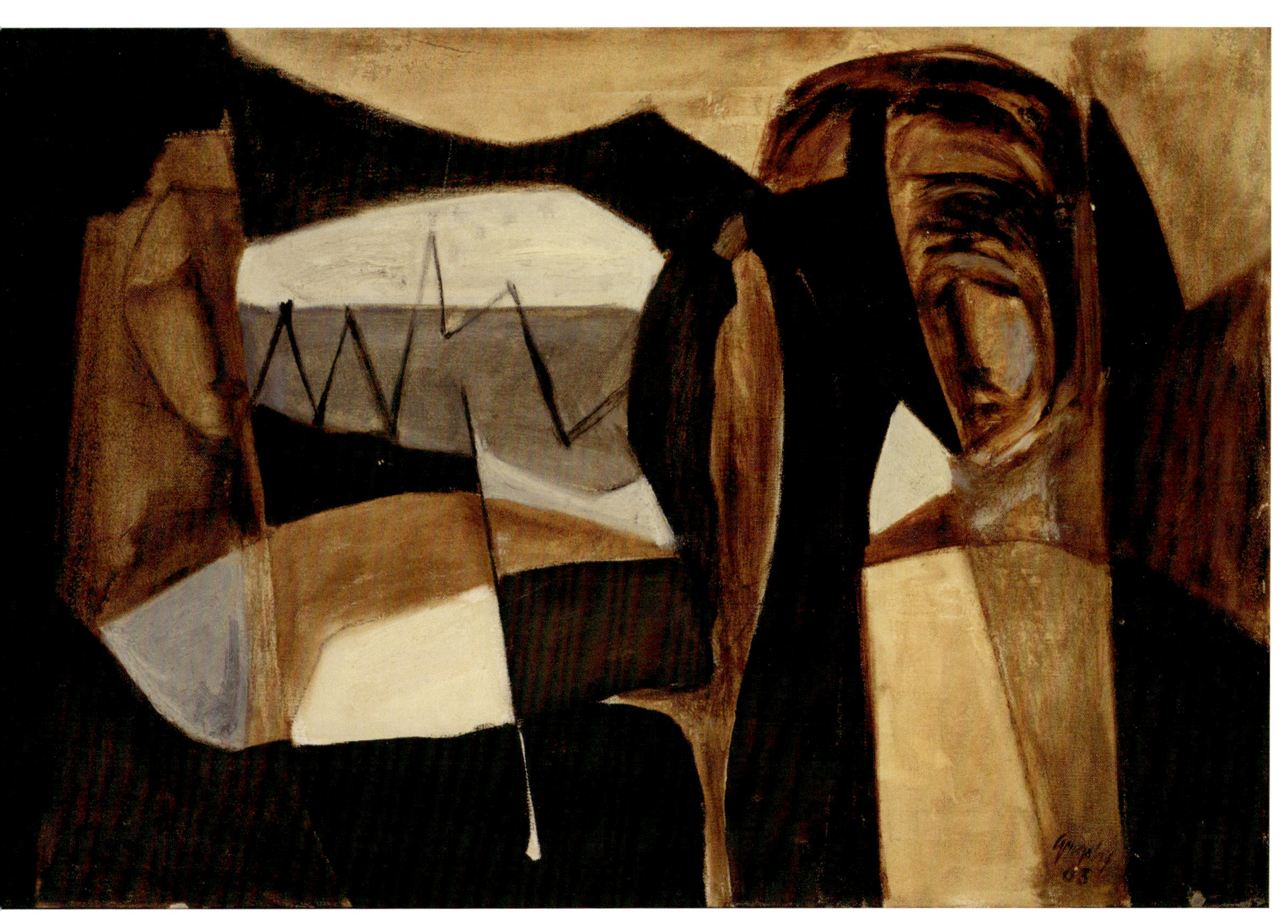

J. EUGENE GRIGSBY

American, 1918–2013

The Enchantress, c. 1979

lithograph on paper

20 ¼ × 15 in.

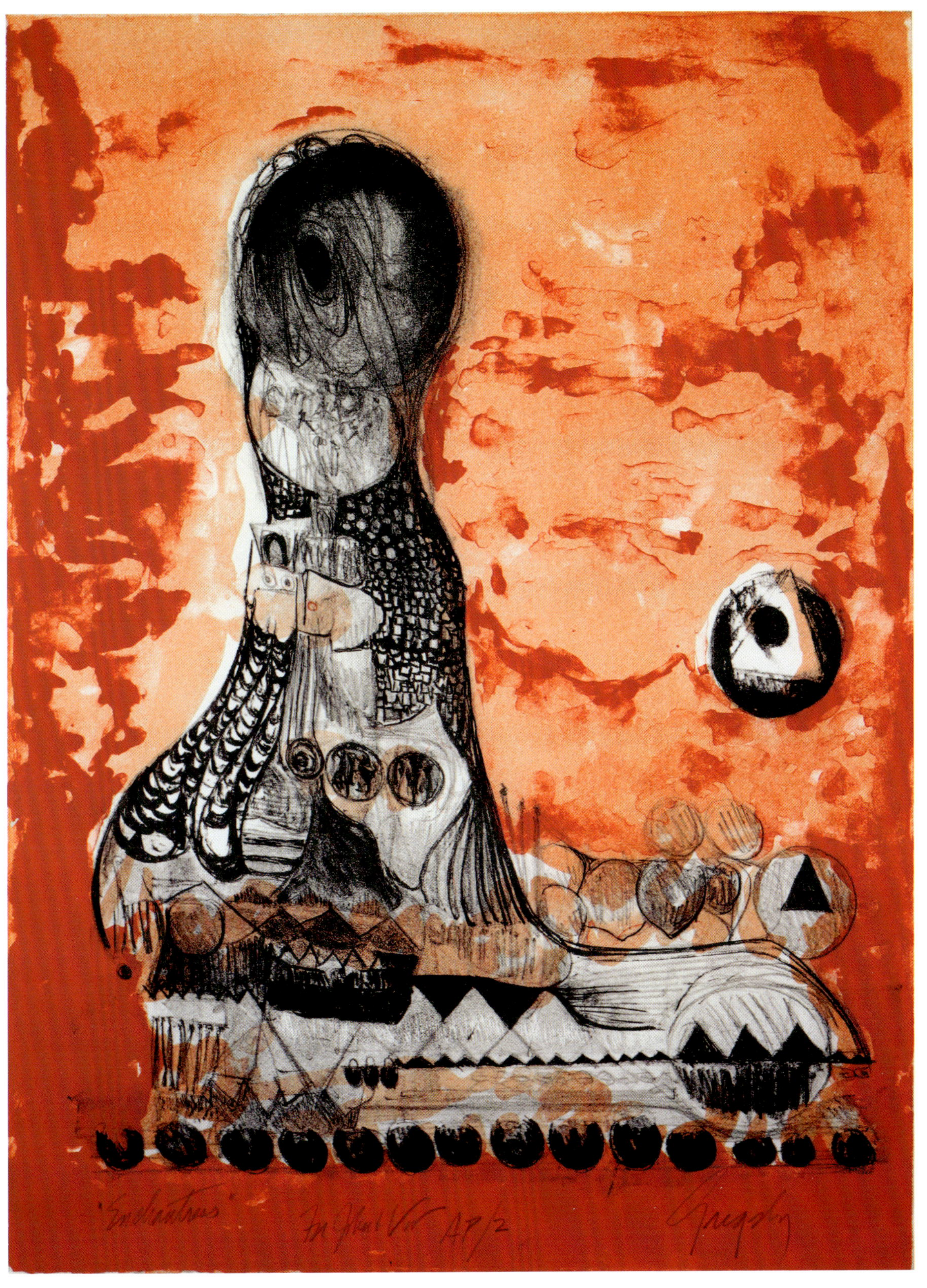
"Enchantress"
AP/2
Gregory

J. EUGENE GRIGSBY
American, 1918–2013
Inner View, c. 1978
lithograph on paper
26 × 19 in.

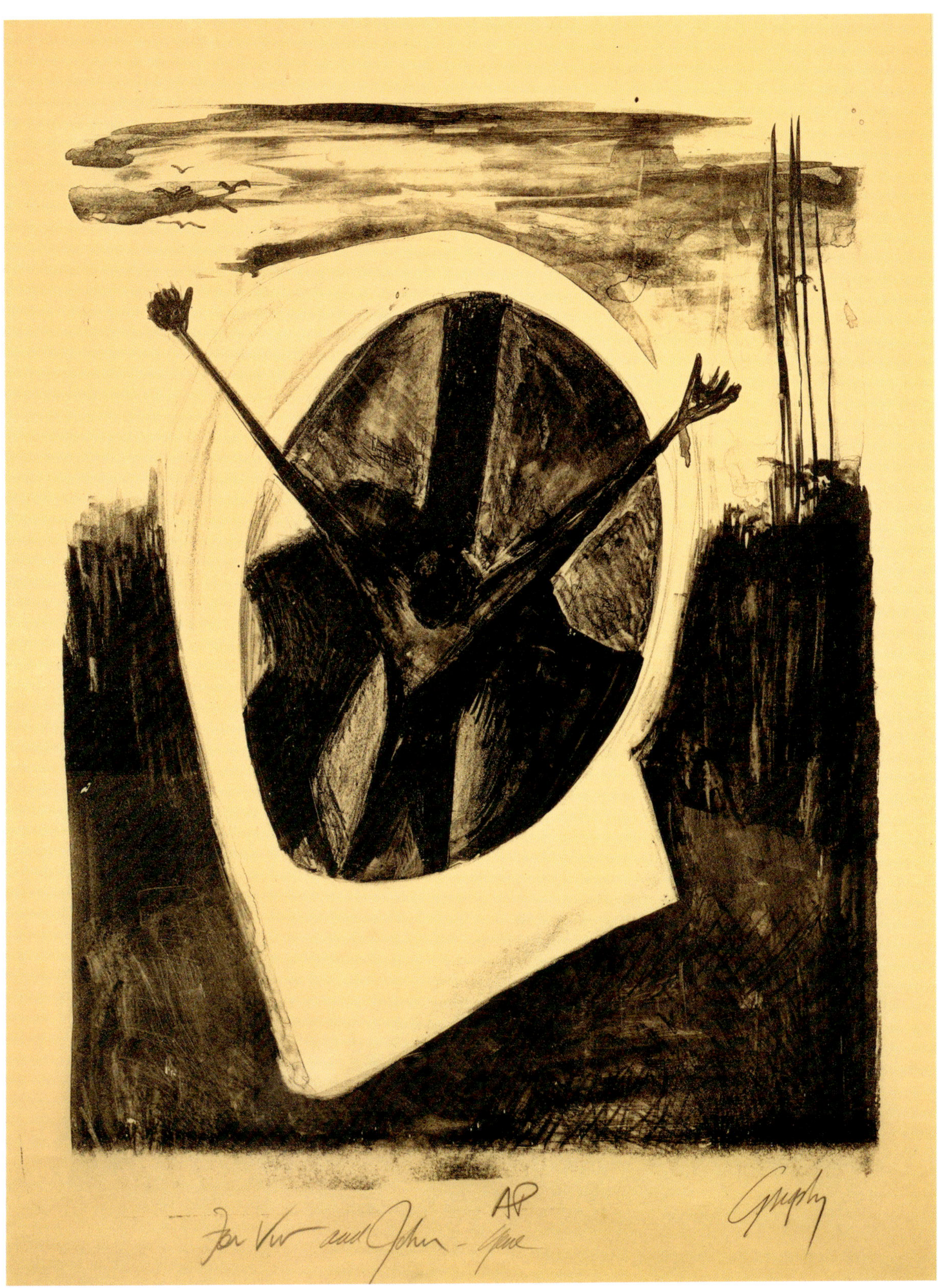
AP
For Viv and John - Gene

J. EUGENE GRIGSBY

American, 1918–2013

No Vacancy, c. 1979

woodcut on paper

21 ¾ × 16 ½ in.

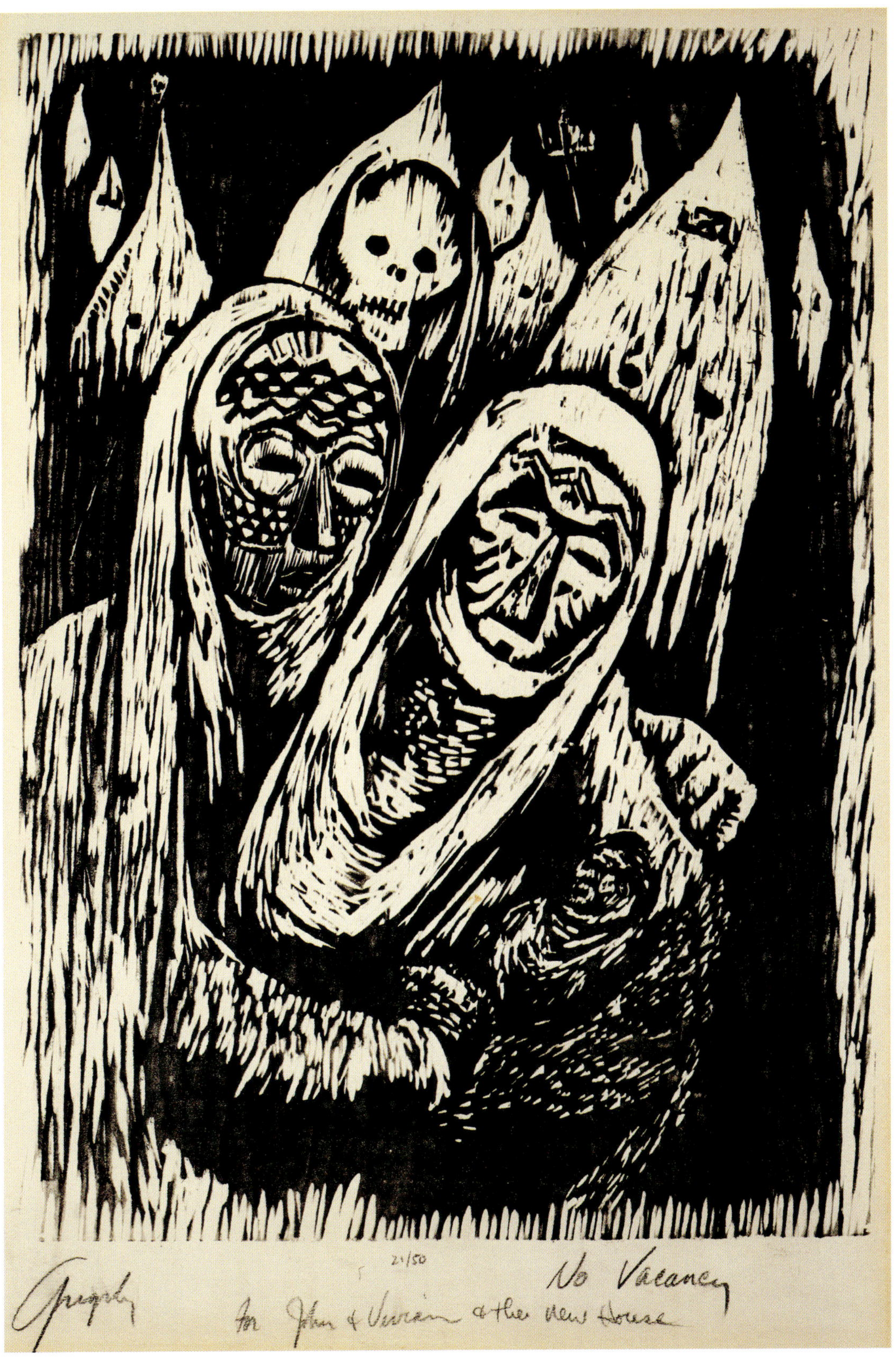
21/50
No Vacancy
for John & Vivian & their new House

J. EUGENE GRIGSBY
American, 1918–2013
Specters, 1970
oil on canvas
17 × 22 in.

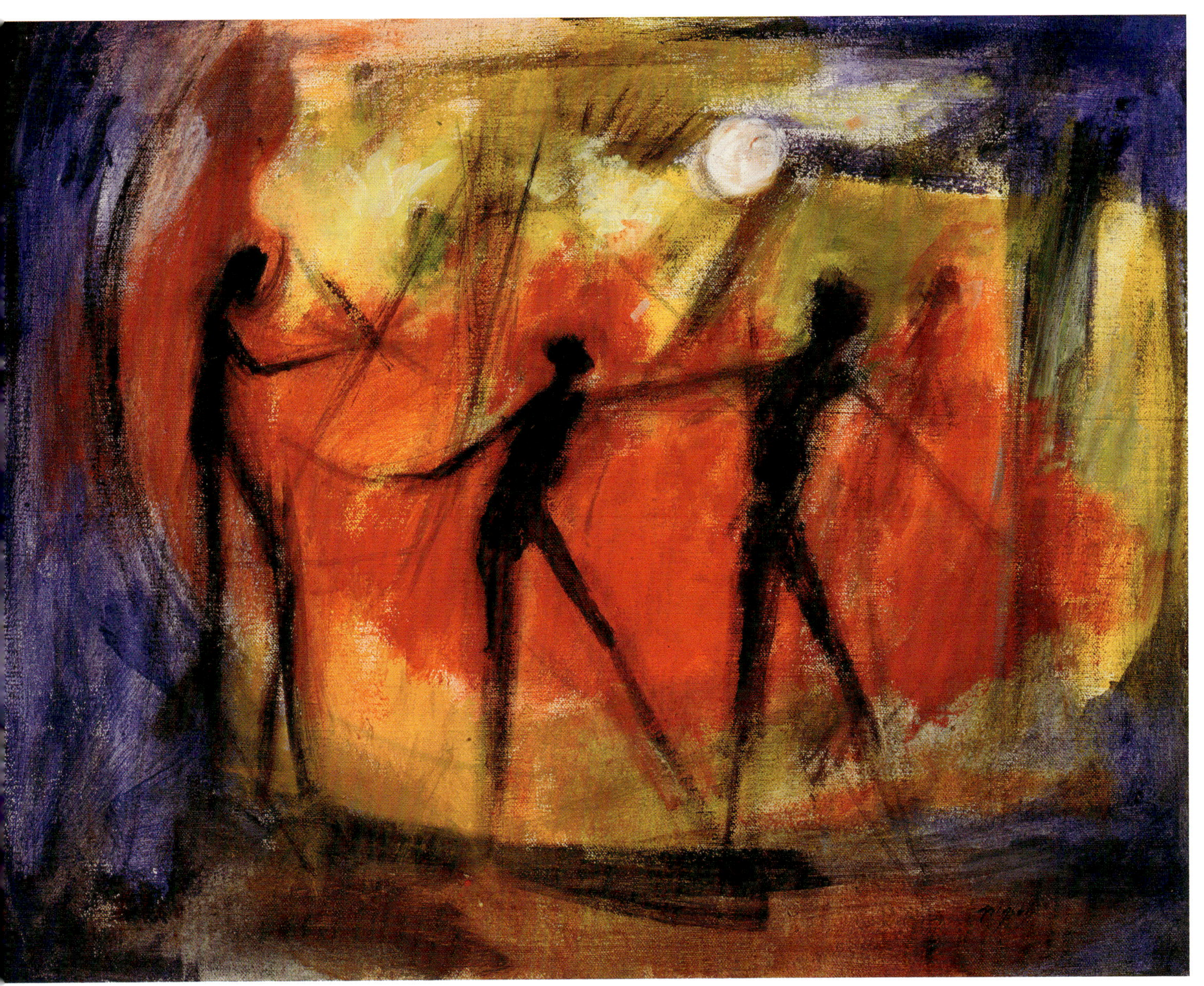

EARL HILL

American, 1927–1985

Beulah's World, 1968

oil on board

24 × 30 in.

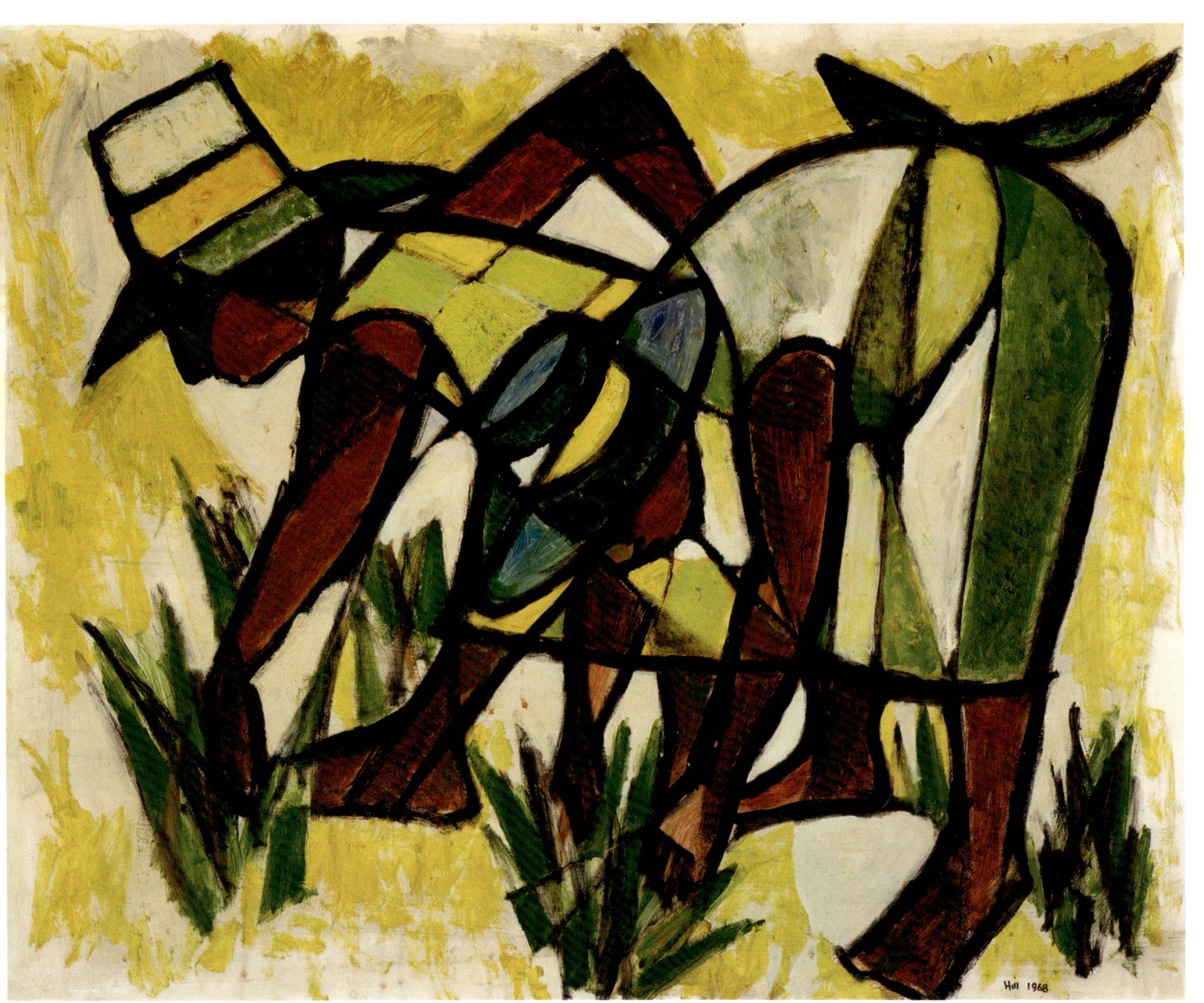
Hill 1968

EARL HILL
American, 1927–1985
The Presence, 1974
oil on wood panel
20 × 7 in.

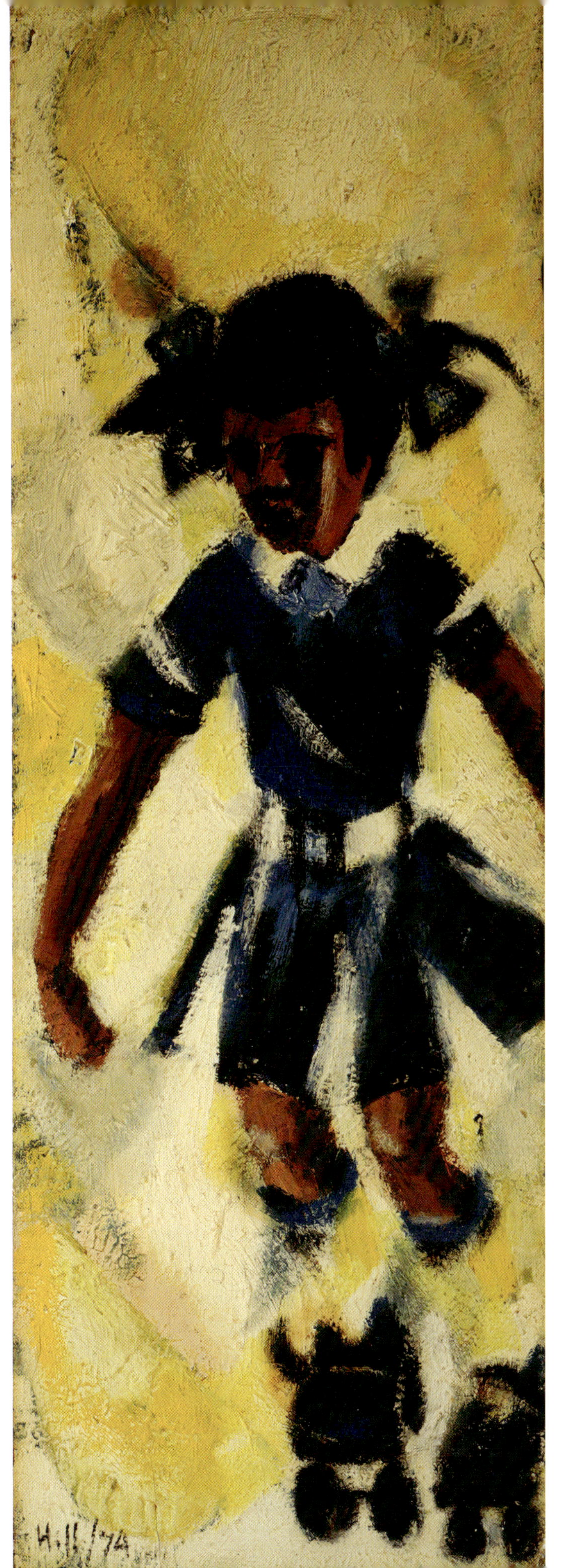

EARL HILL

American, 1927–1985
Weight of the World, 1967
watercolor and graphite on paper
9 ½ × 5 ¾ in.

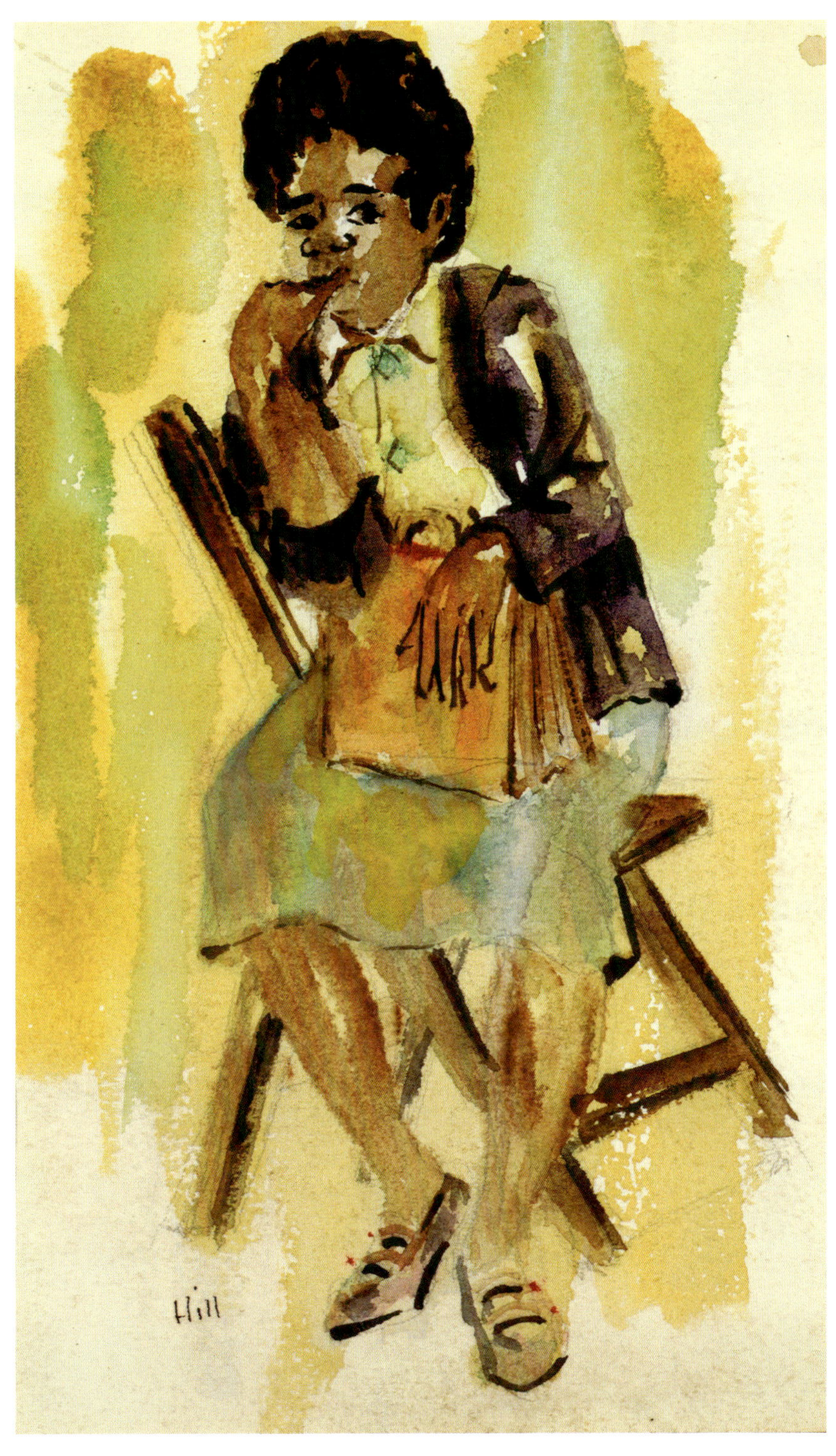
Hill

ALVIN C. HOLLINGSWORTH

American, 1928–2000

African Village, c. 1978

oil and india ink on canvas board

13 × 17 in.

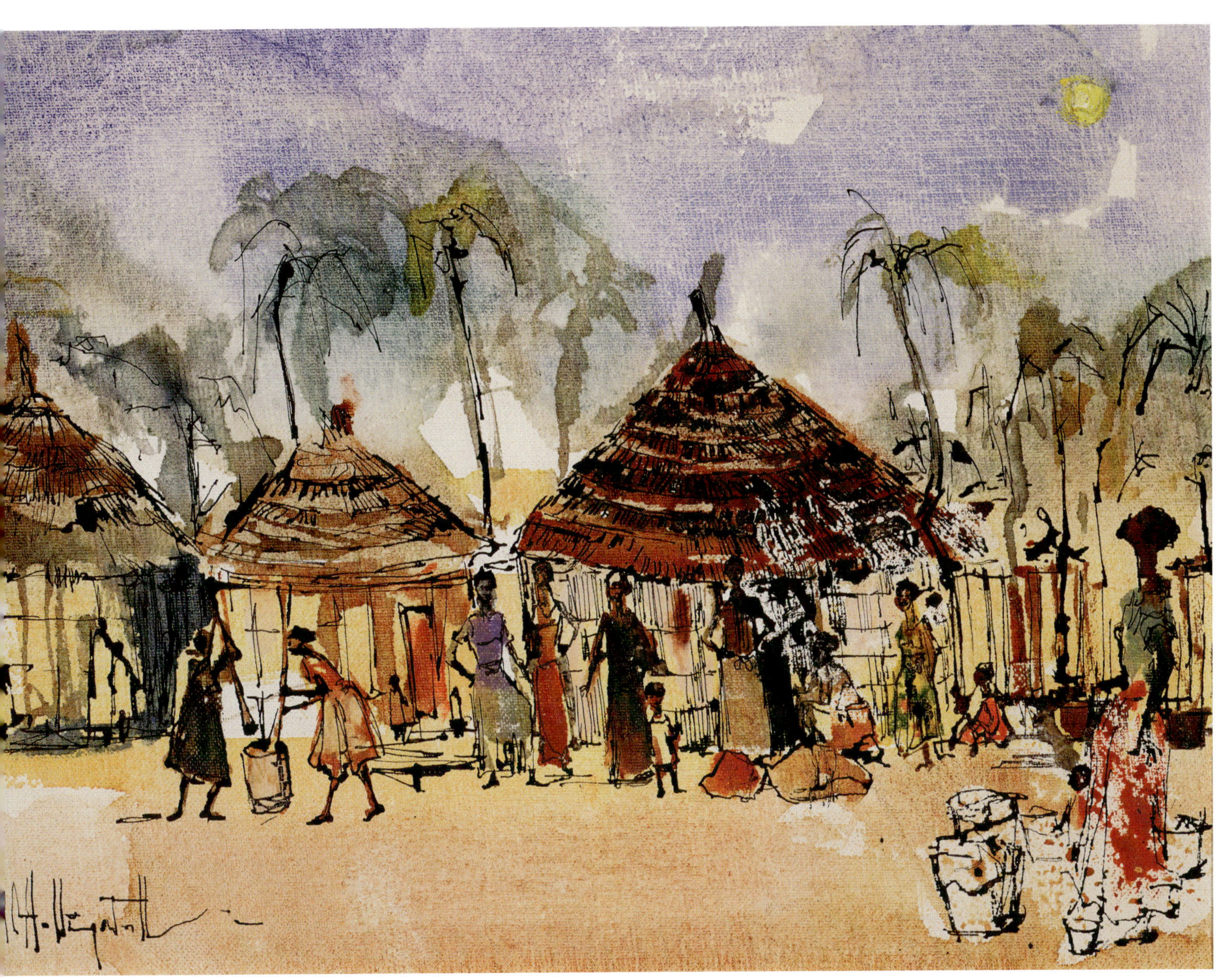

ALVIN C. HOLLINGSWORTH

American, 1928–2000
Family Tree, c. 1977
lithograph on paper
26 × 22 in.

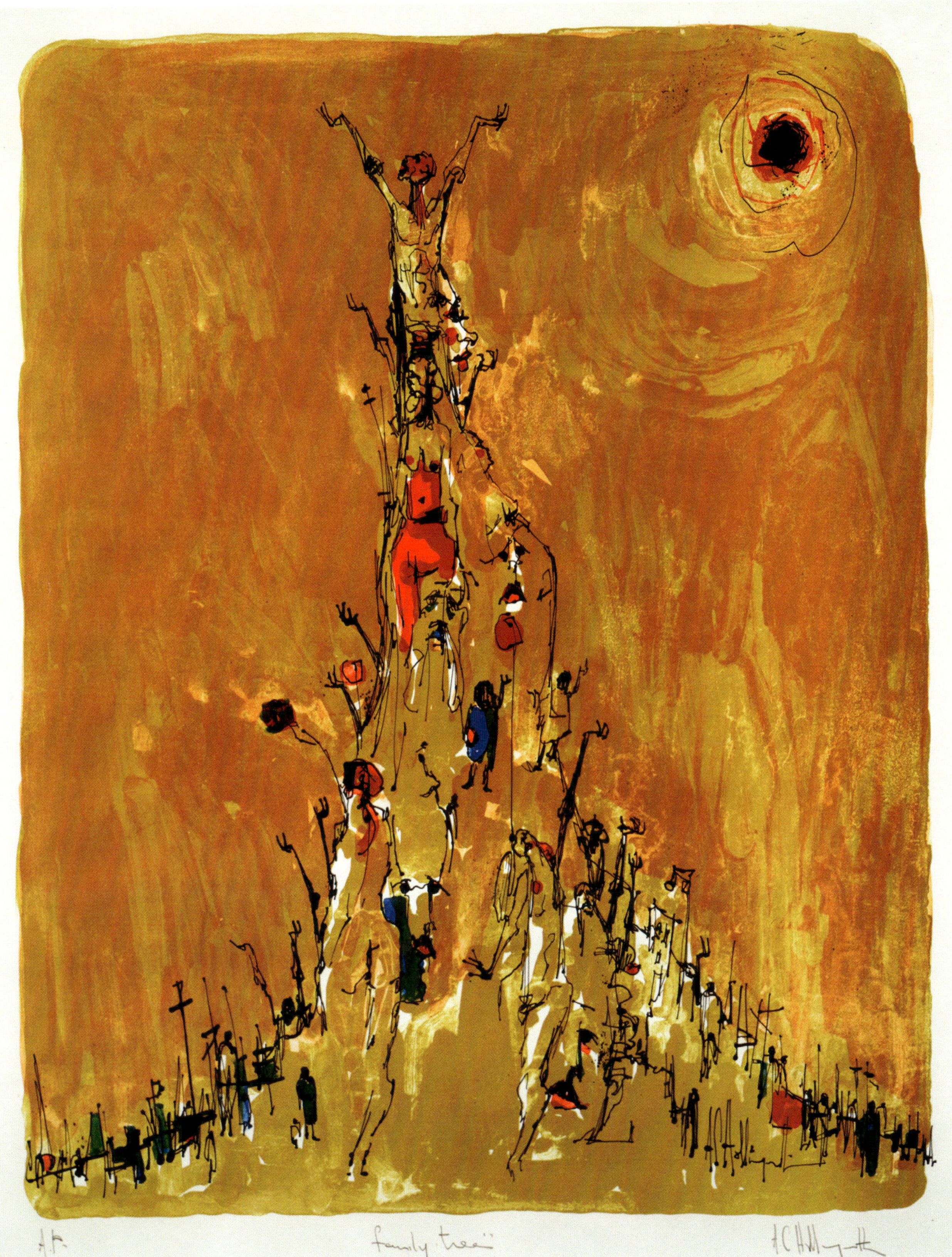
family tree

ALVIN C. HOLLINGSWORTH

American, 1928–2000

Tomorrow, c. 1977

oil and india ink on canvas board

15 × 12 in.

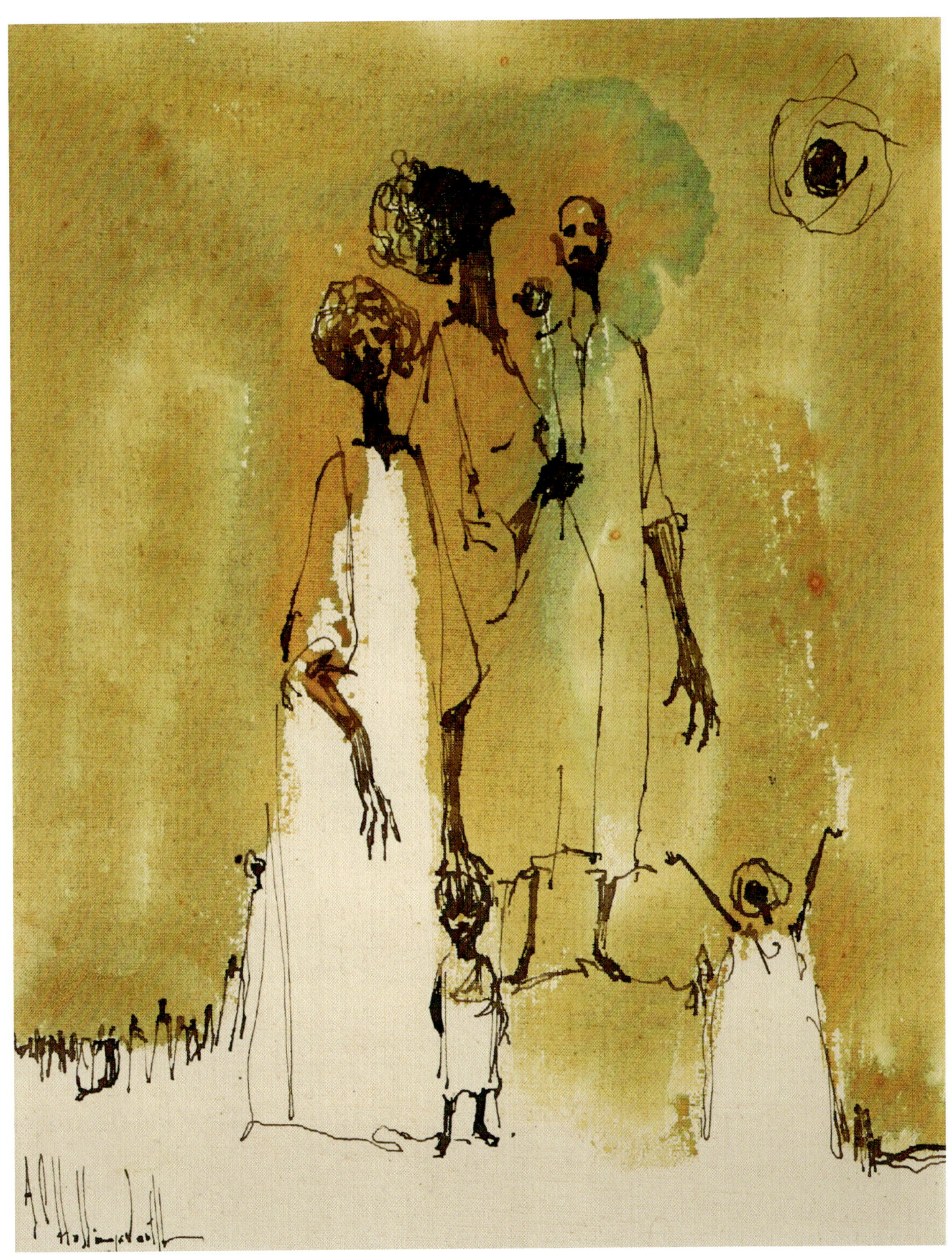

ALVIN C. HOLLINGSWORTH

American, 1928–2000
Waiting #2, c. 1977
oil, acrylic, and collage on canvas
12 × 9 in.

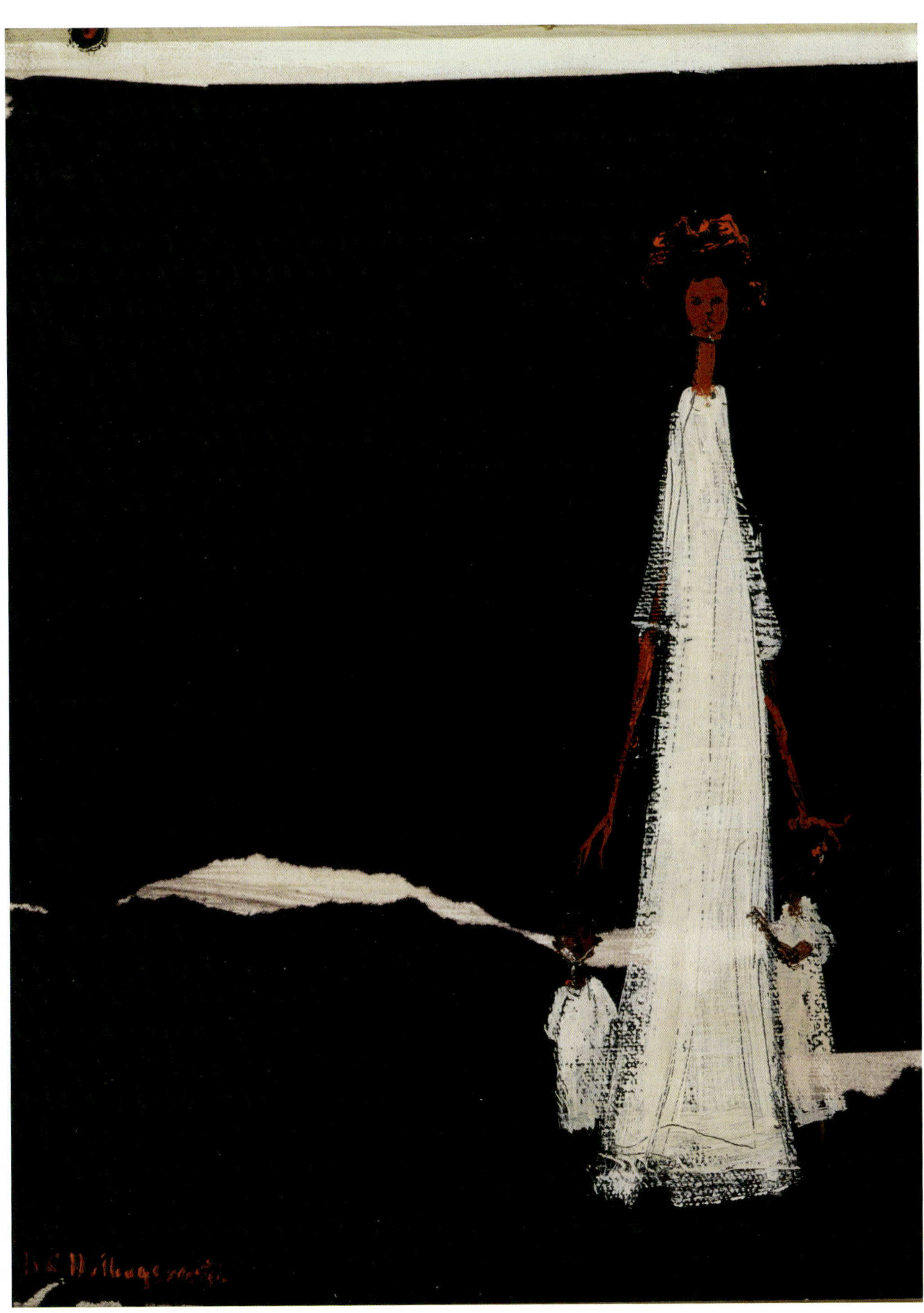

RONALD JOSEPH

American, b. British West Indies, 1910–1992; active Belgium, 1956–1992

Two Musicians, n.d.

lithograph on paper

32 × 24 in.

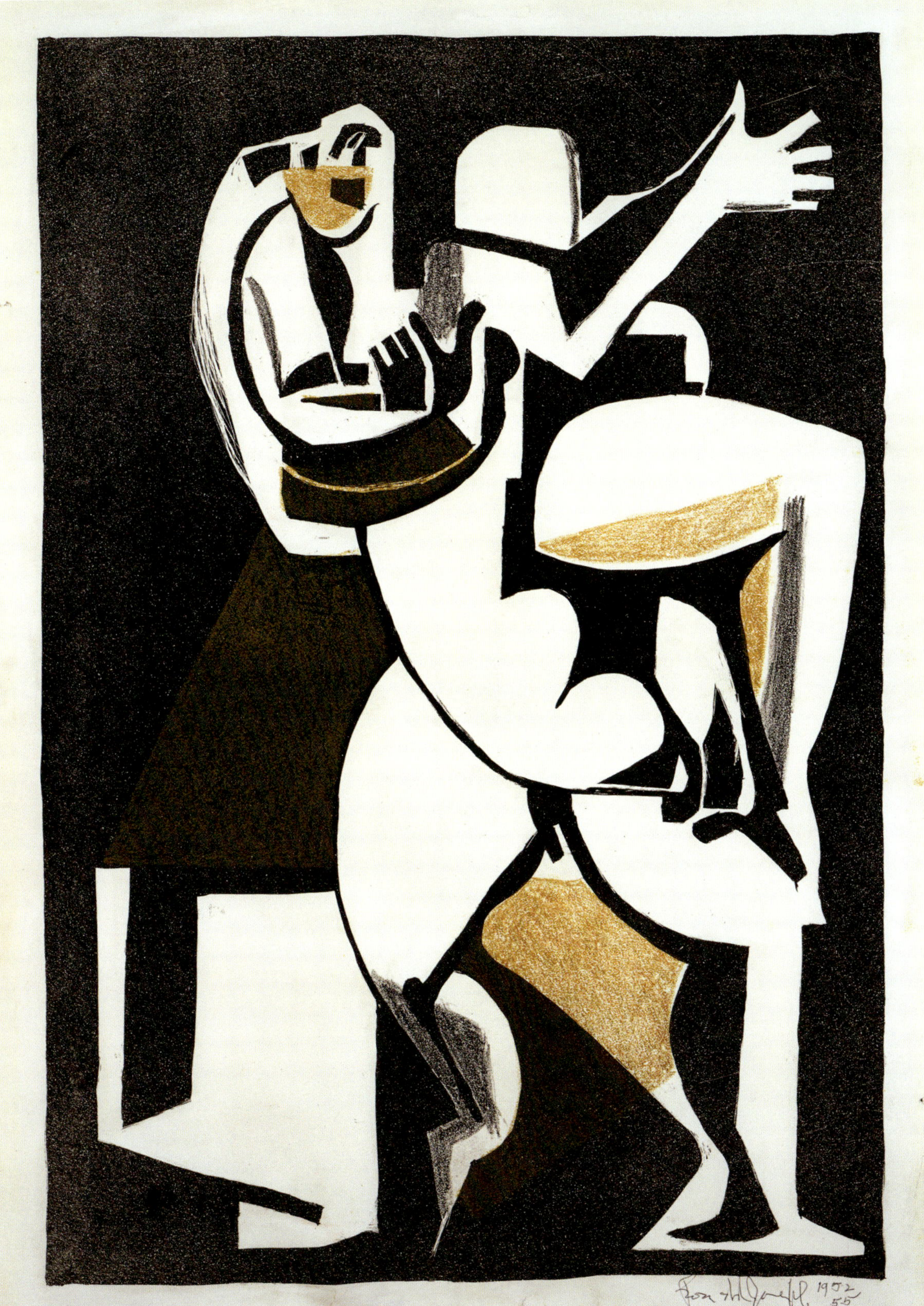

RONALD JOSEPH

American, b. British West Indies, 1910–1992; active Belgium, 1956–1992

The Family, c. 1953

colored pencil and gouache on paper

23 ¾ × 18 7/8 in.

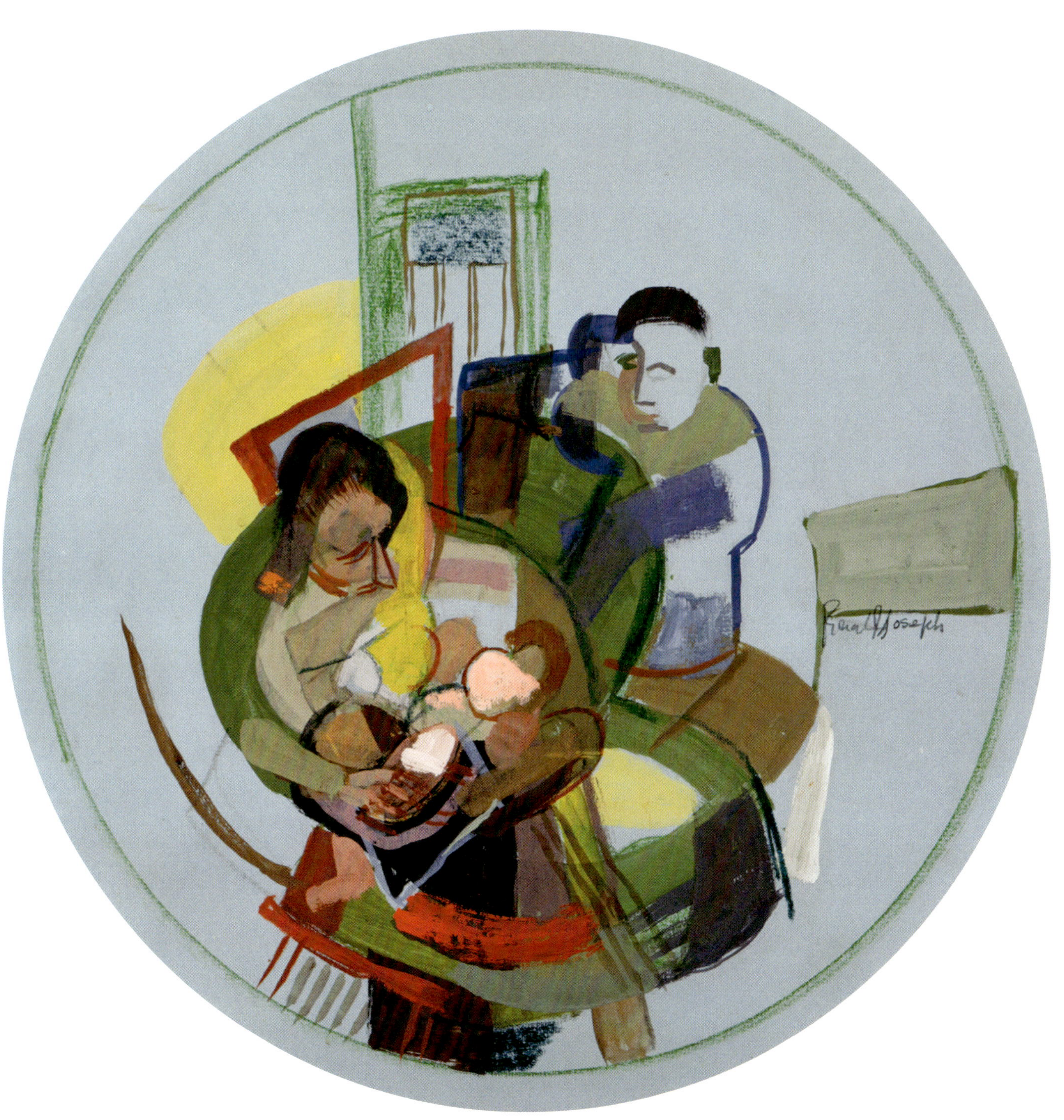

RONALD JOSEPH

American, b. British West Indies, 1910–1992; active Belgium, 1956–1992

Still Life, n.d.

gouache and charcoal on paper

17 ½ × 22 in.

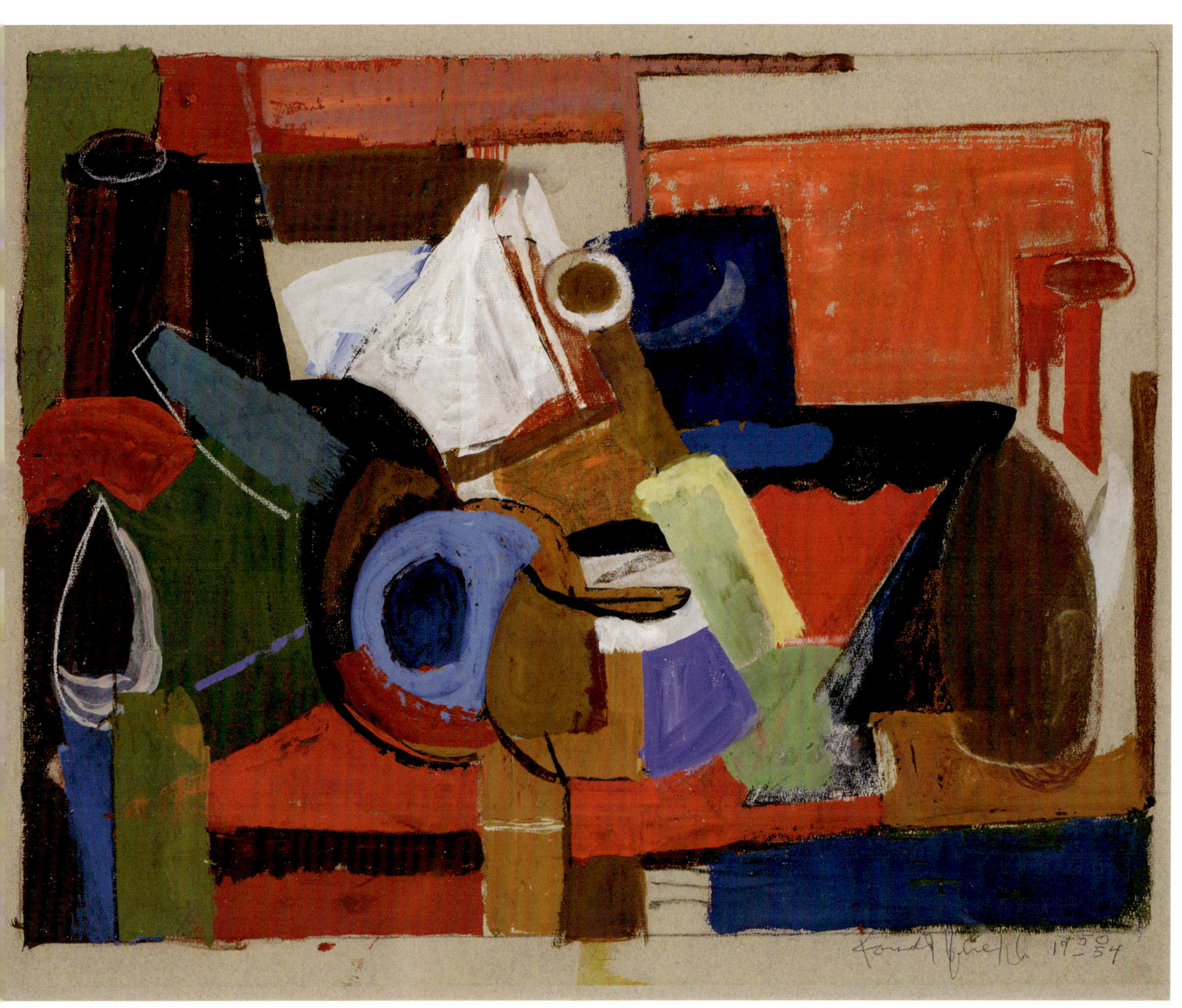

JACOB LAWRENCE
American, 1917–2000
Playing Records, 1949
india ink on paper
23 × 18 in.

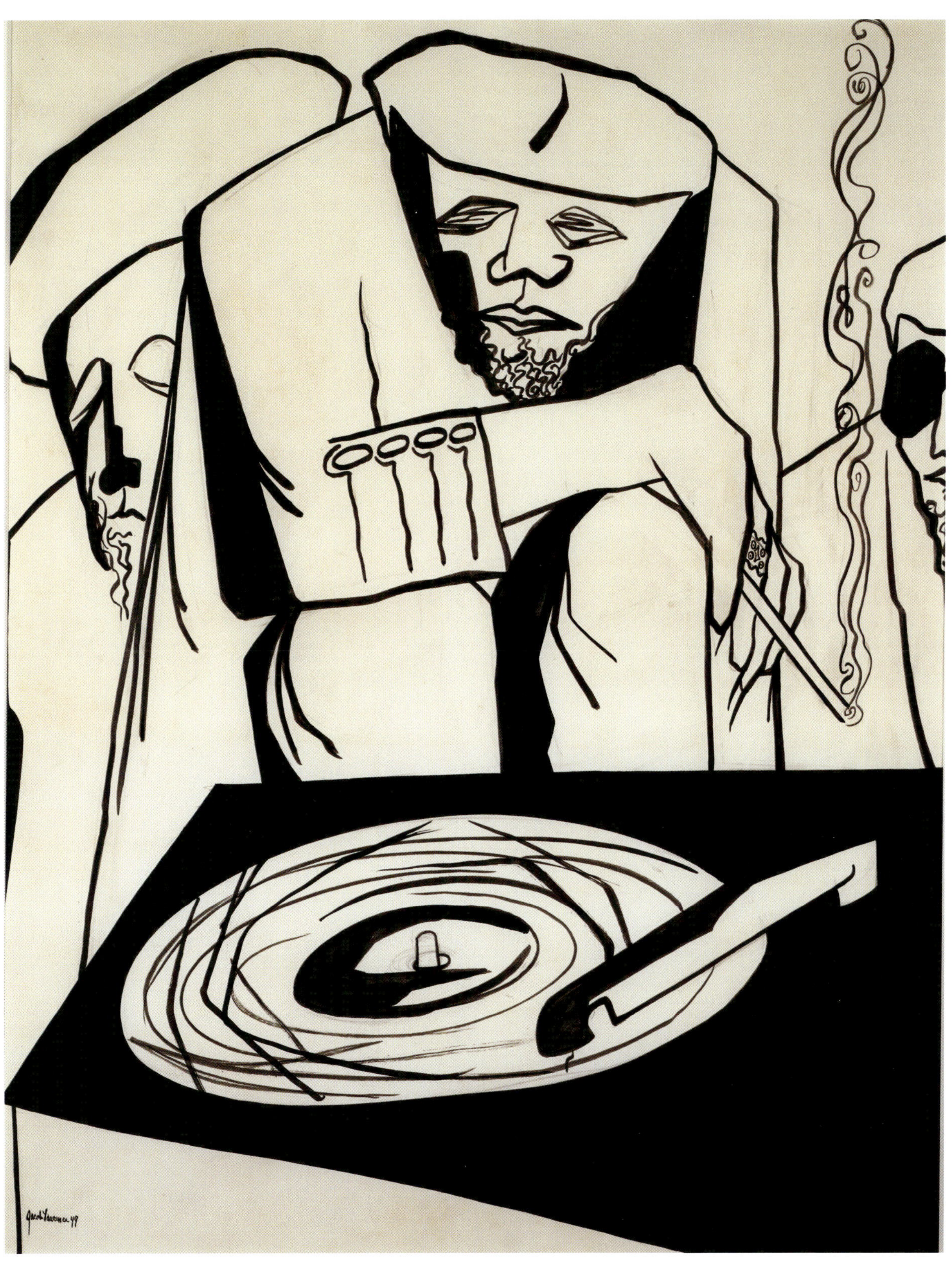

HUGHIE LEE-SMITH

American, 1915–1999

Signaler II, 1983

oil on canvas

9 × 12 in.

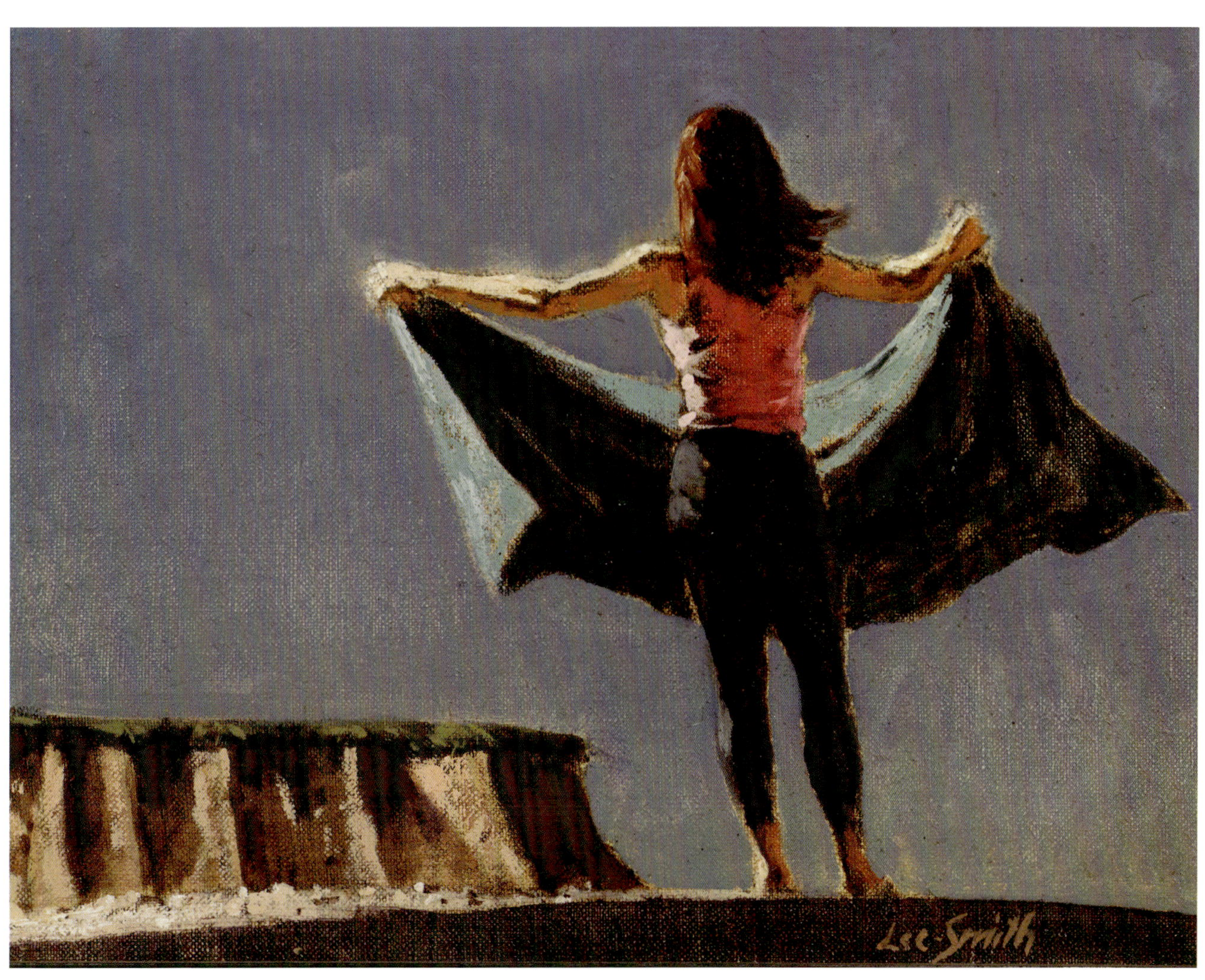
Lee-Smith

VIRGINIA EVANS SMIT

American, b. 1936

Harlem Games, c. 1964

woodcut on paper

20 ½ × 18 ½ in.

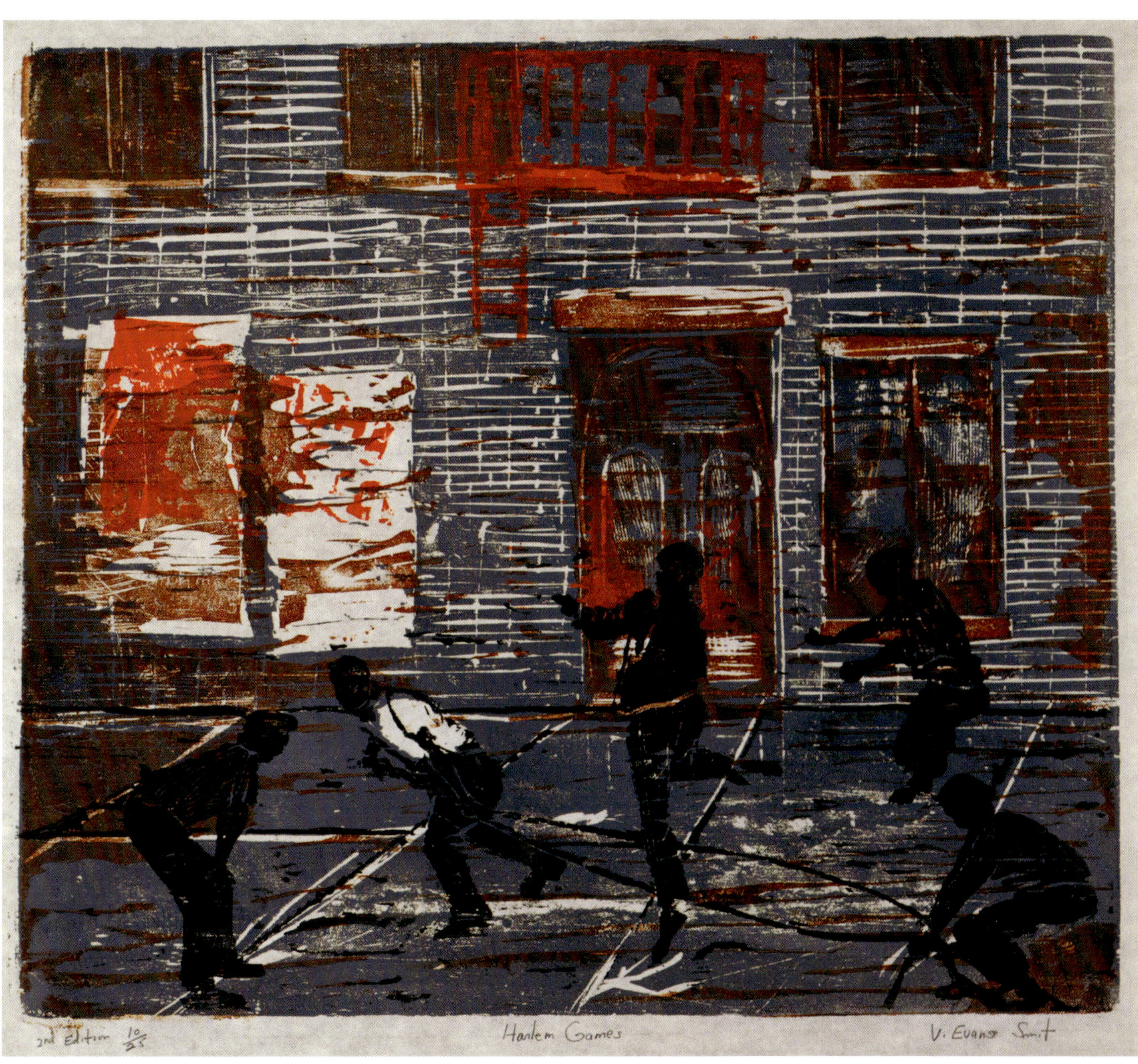
2nd Edition 10/25
Harlem Games
V. Evans Smit

ANN TANKSLEY

American, b. 1934

Canal Builders II, 1989

oil on linen

36 × 25 ½ in.

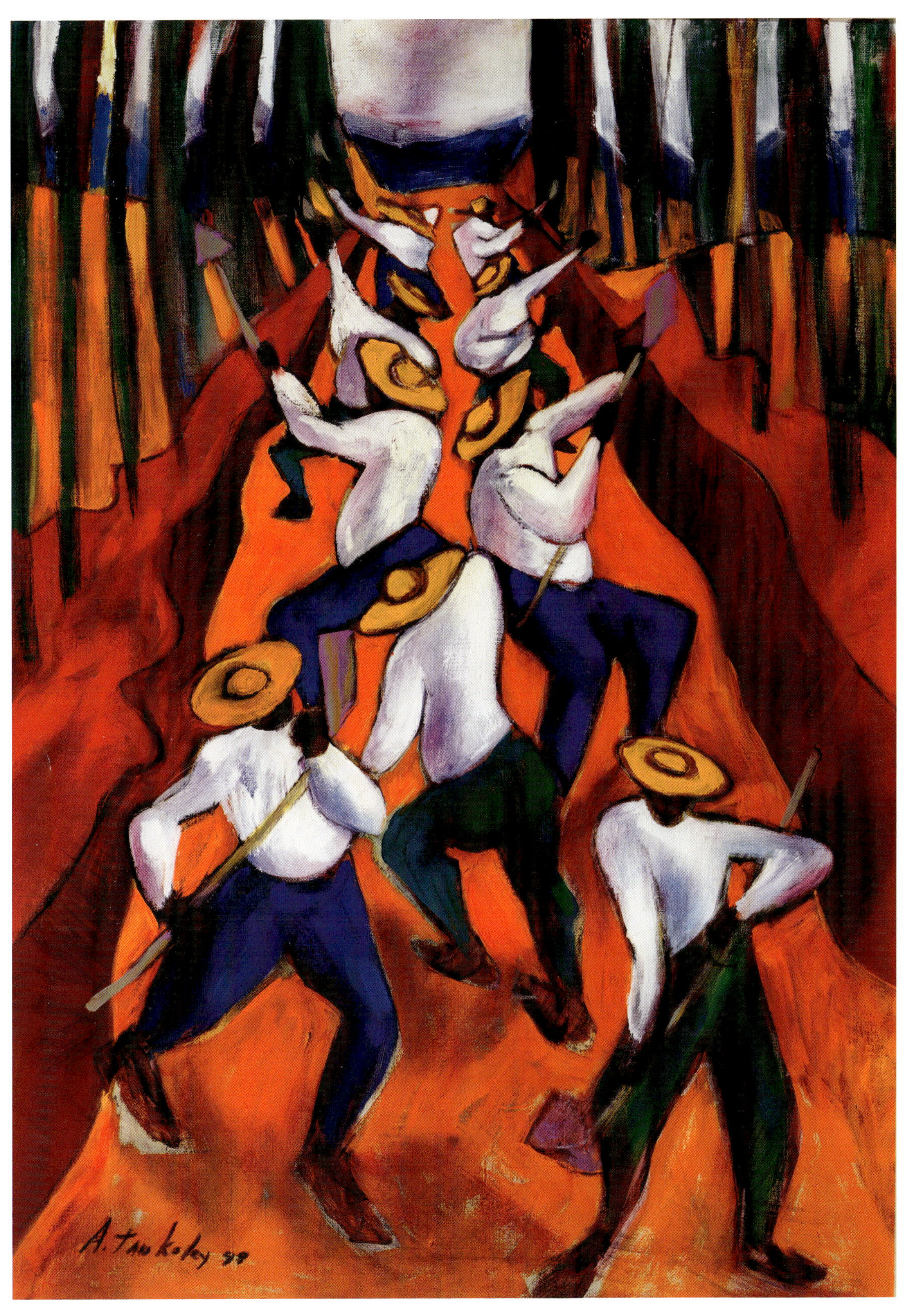

ANN TANKSLEY
American, b. 1934
Harvest of Shame, 1979
oil on composition board
24 × 18 in.

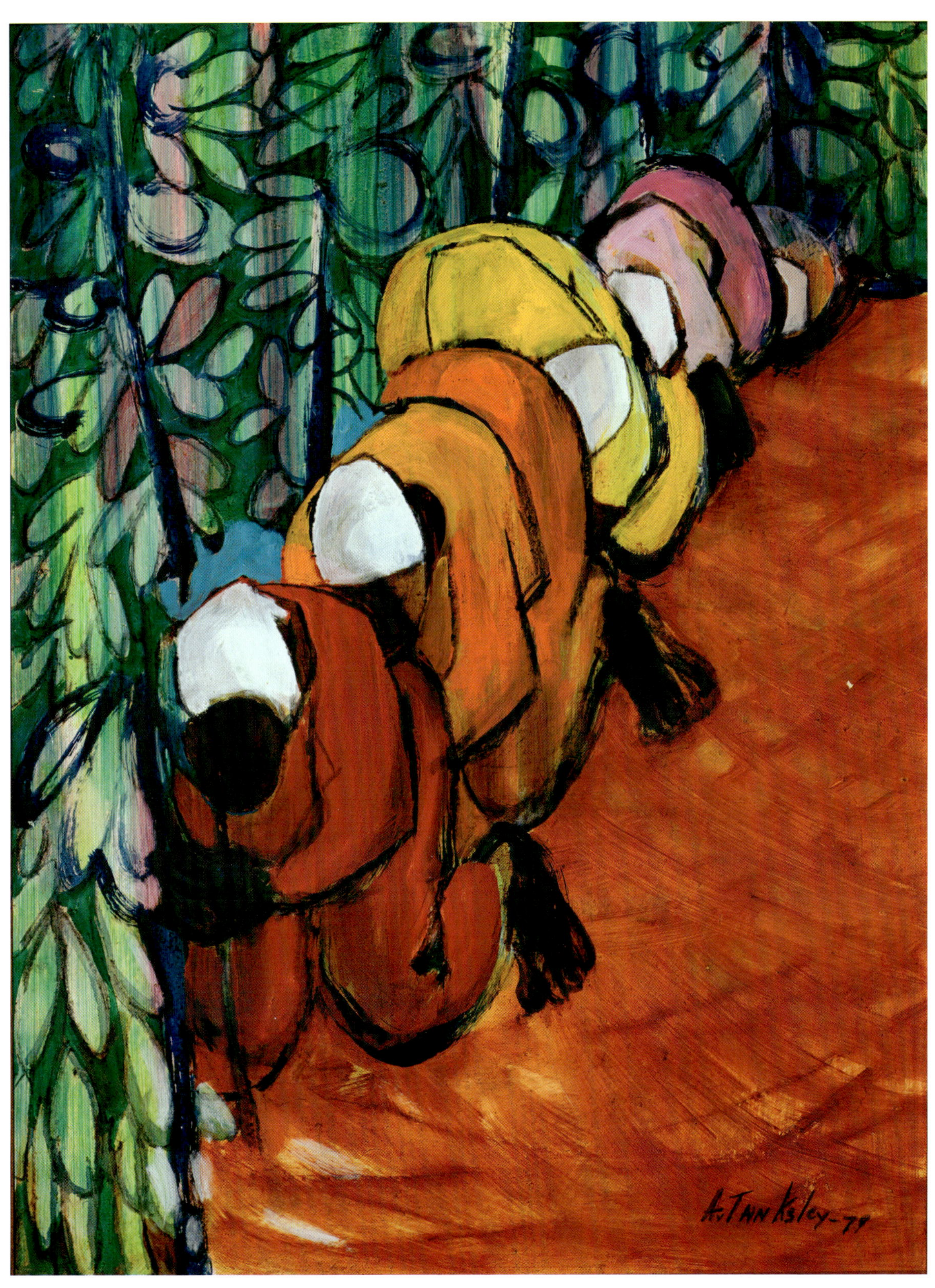
A. TANKsley-79

ANN TANKSLEY
American, b. 1934
New Wave, 1987
monotype on paper
10 ½ × 6 in.

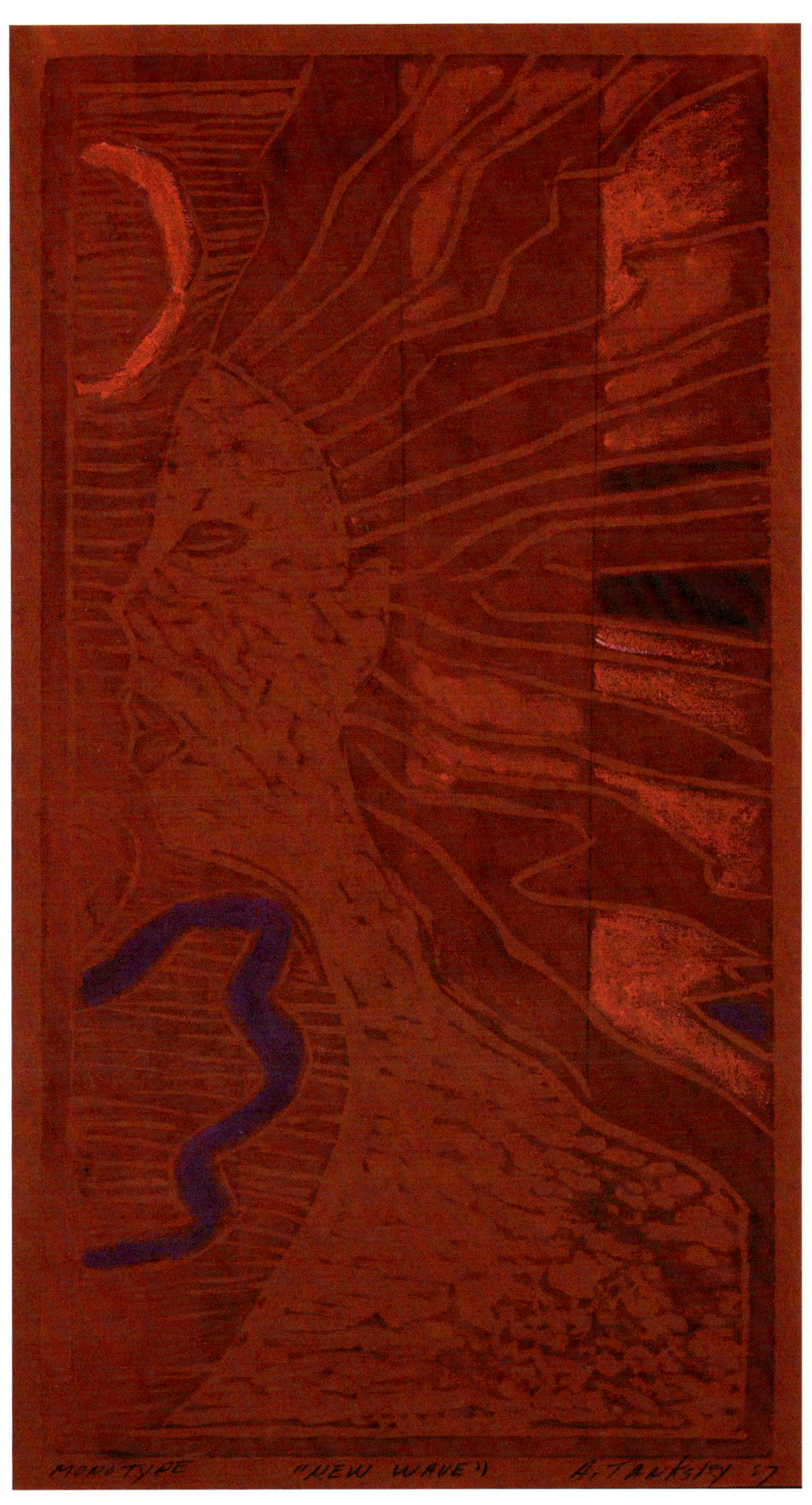
MONOTYPE
"NEW WAVE"
A. TANKSLEY 57

HENRY OSSAWA TANNER

American, 1859–1937; active France, 1899–1937

Gate in Tangiers, c. 1910

oil on canvas

18 ¼ × 15 in.

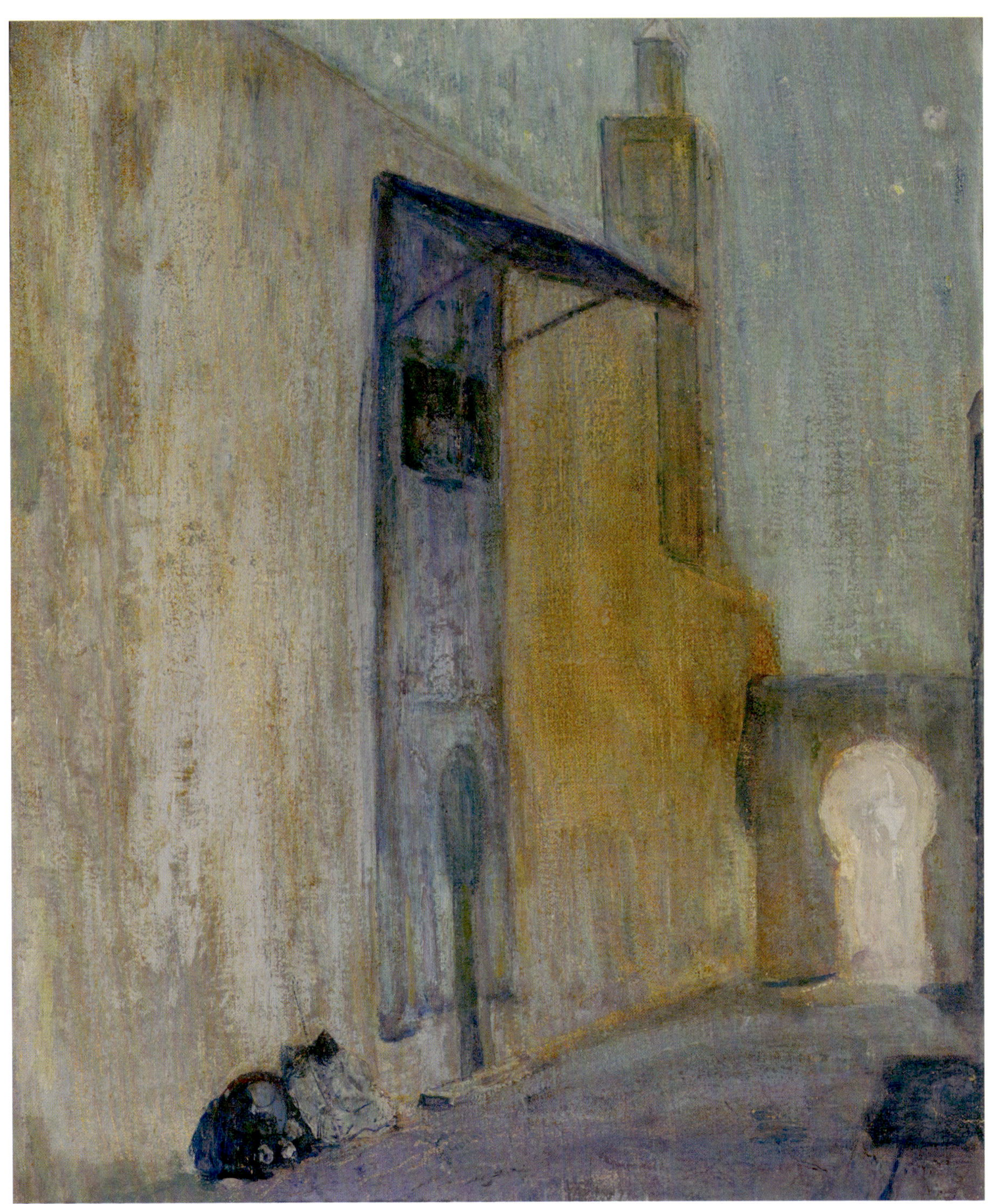

HENRY OSSAWA TANNER

American, 1859–1937; active France, 1899–1937

Seated Figure, c. 1900

graphite on paper

9 ½ × 9 ¼ in.

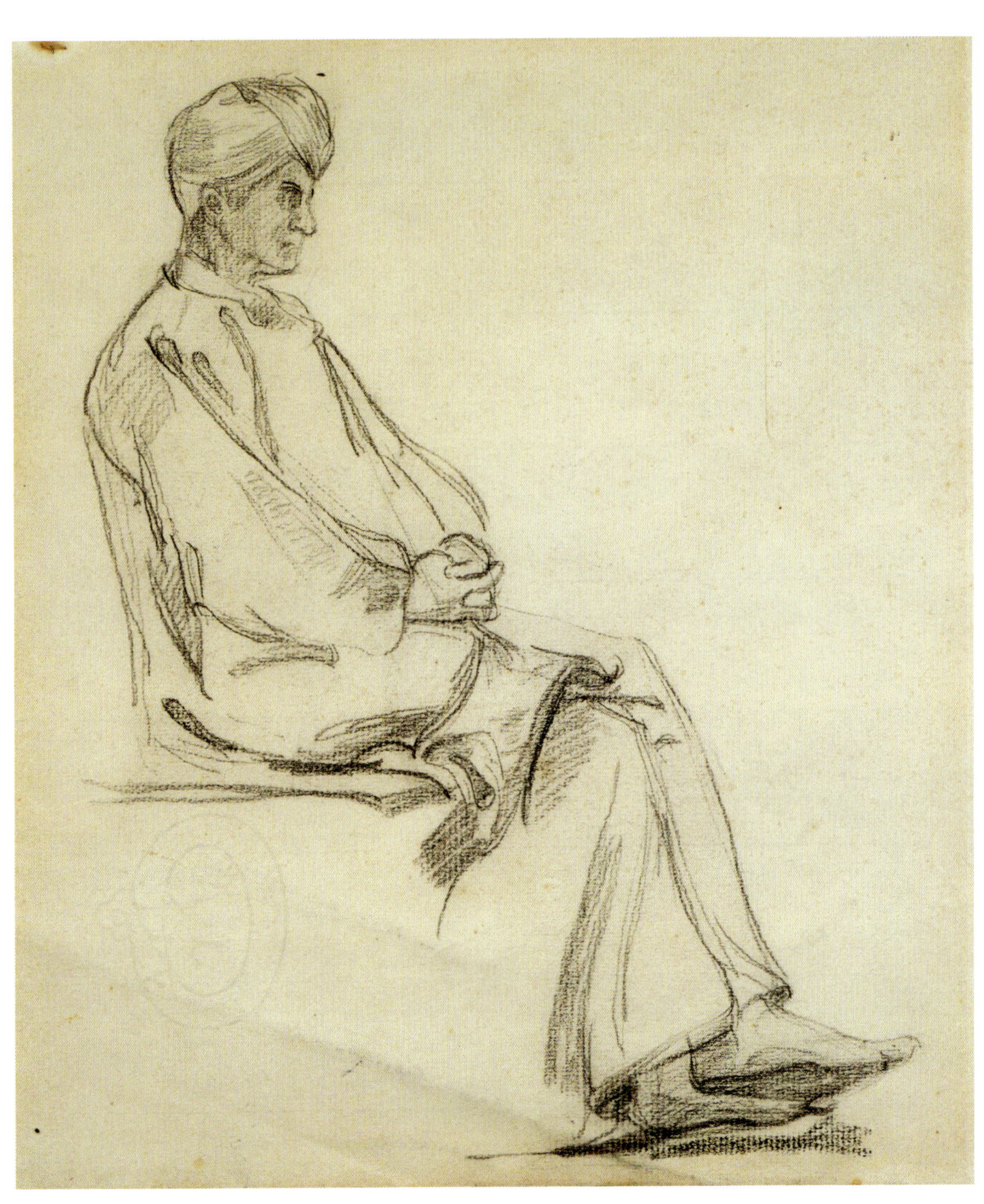

HENRY OSSAWA TANNER

American, 1859–1937; active France, 1899–1937

Head of a Man (recto), c. 1900

conté crayon on paper

9 ¼ × 8 ¾ in.

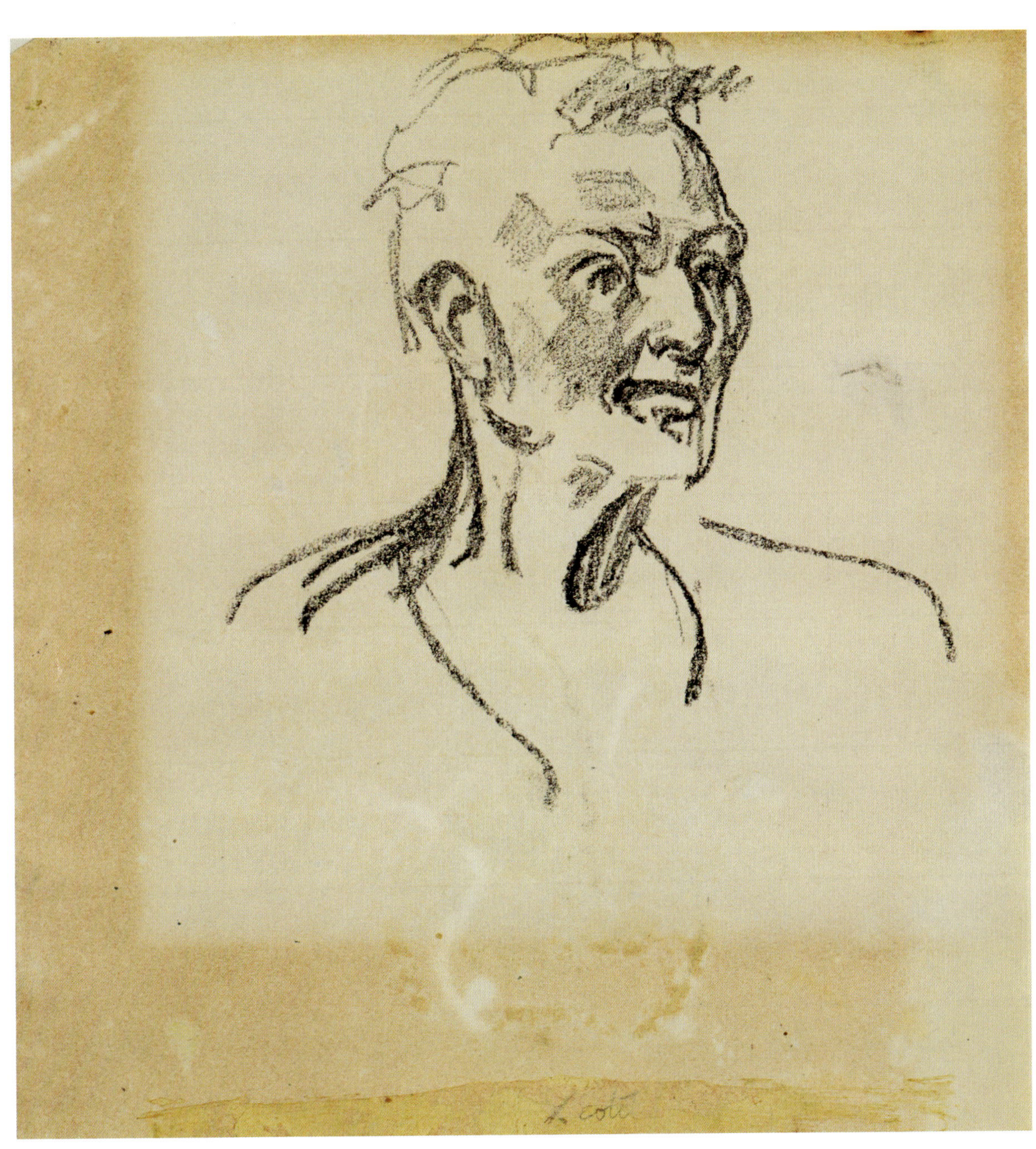

HENRY OSSAWA TANNER

American, 1859–1937; active France, 1899–1937

Head of a Man (verso), c. 1900

conté crayon on paper

9 ¼ × 8 ¾ in.

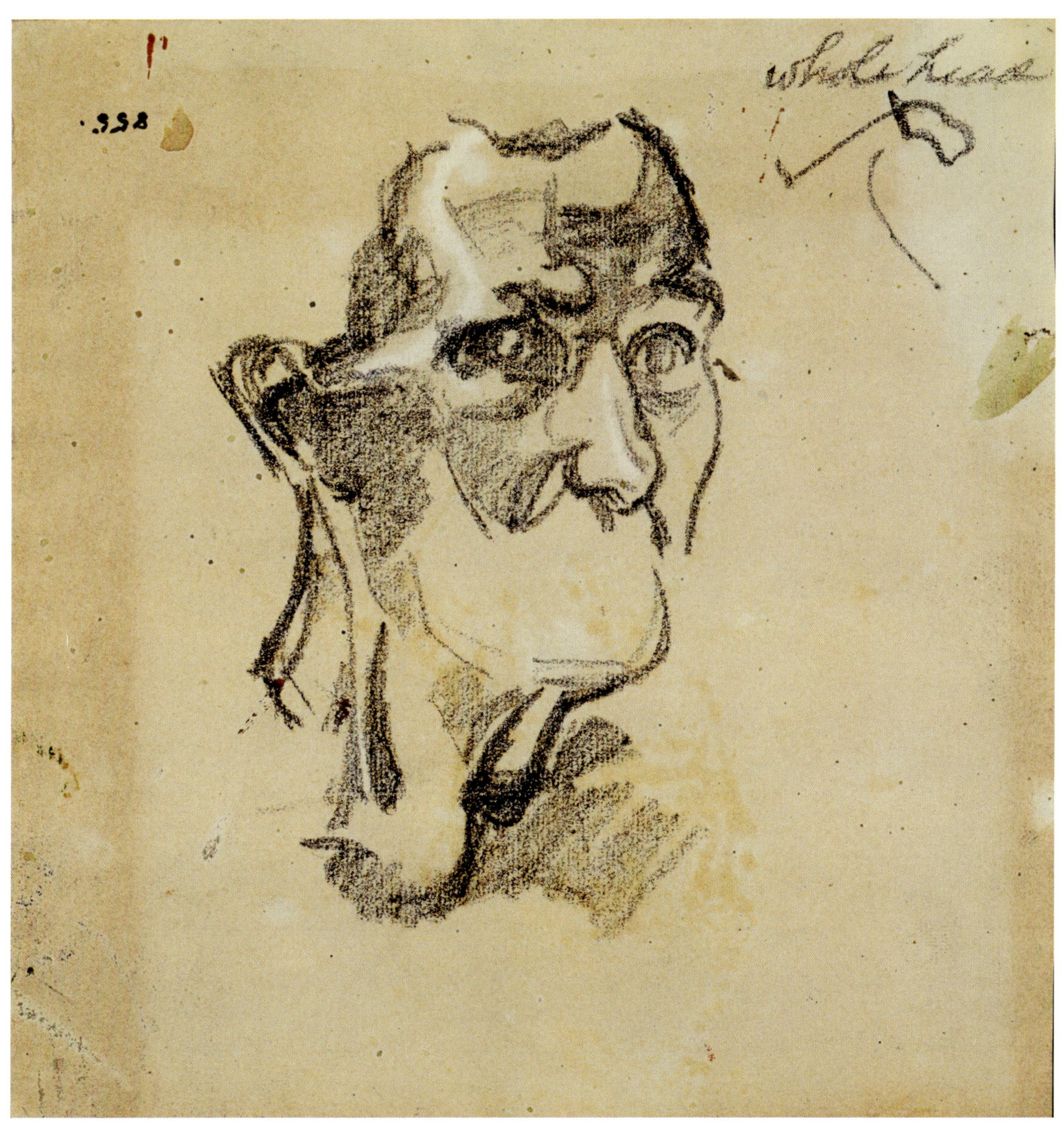
338
whole head

ELLIS WILSON
American, 1899–1977
Haitian Camion, 1953
oil on board
19 ¼ × 29 in.

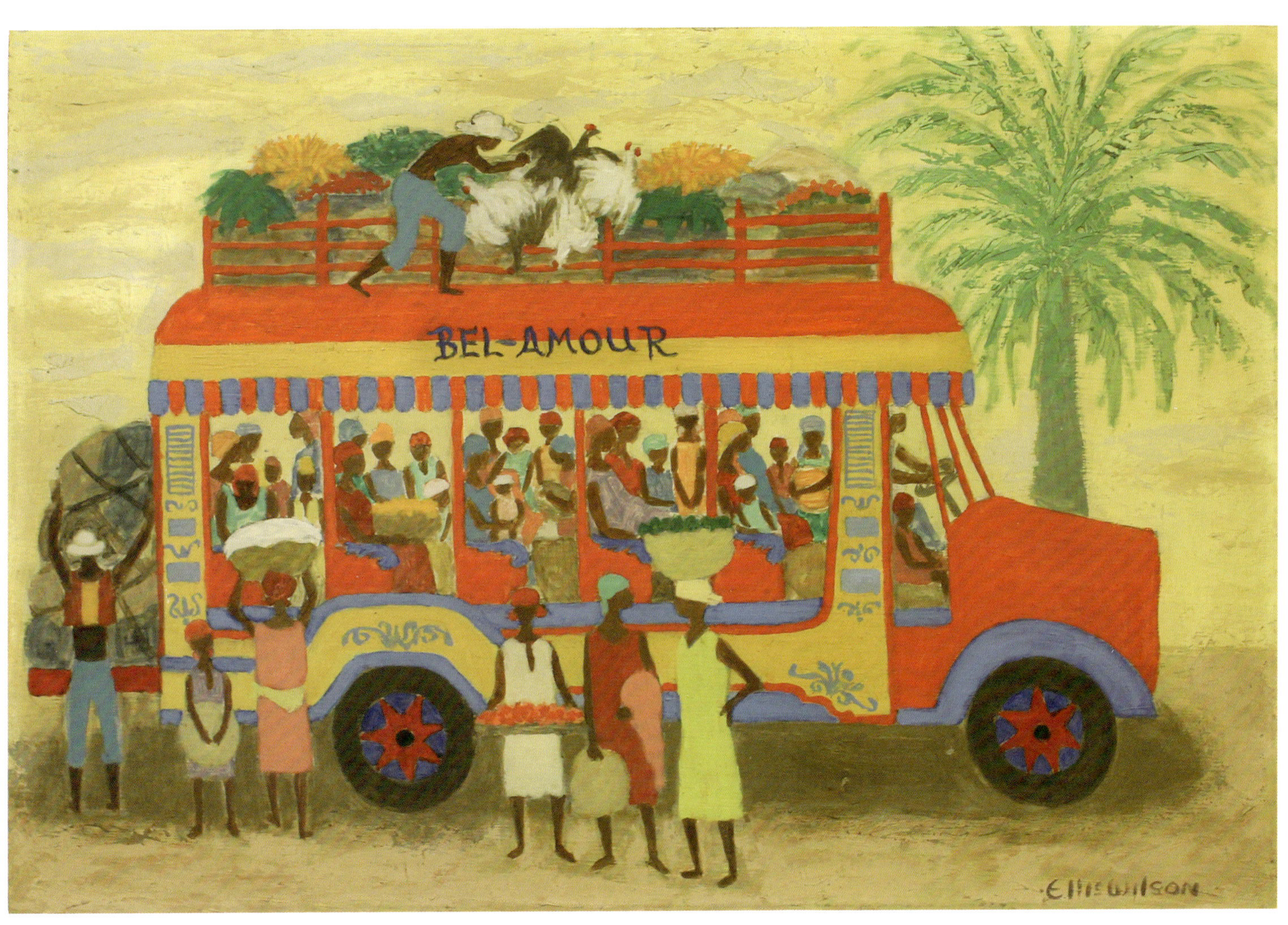
BEL-AMOUR
Ellis Wilson

FRANK WIMBERLEY
American, b. 1926
Seventy-Eight, 1978
collage on paper
19 ½ × 16 in.

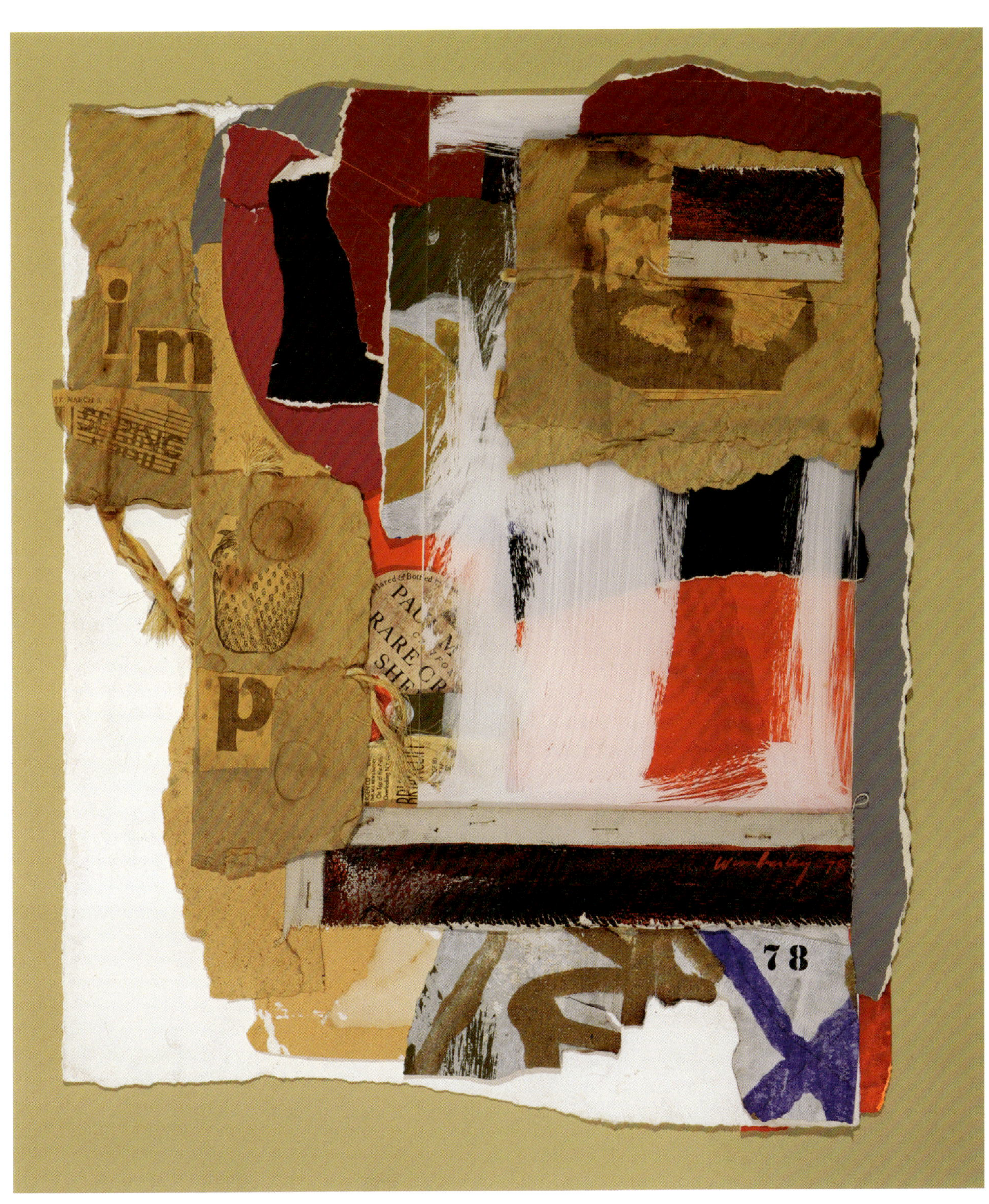
im
p
78

HALE A. WOODRUFF
American, 1900–1980
The Card Players, 1978
oil on canvas
36 × 42 ¼ in.

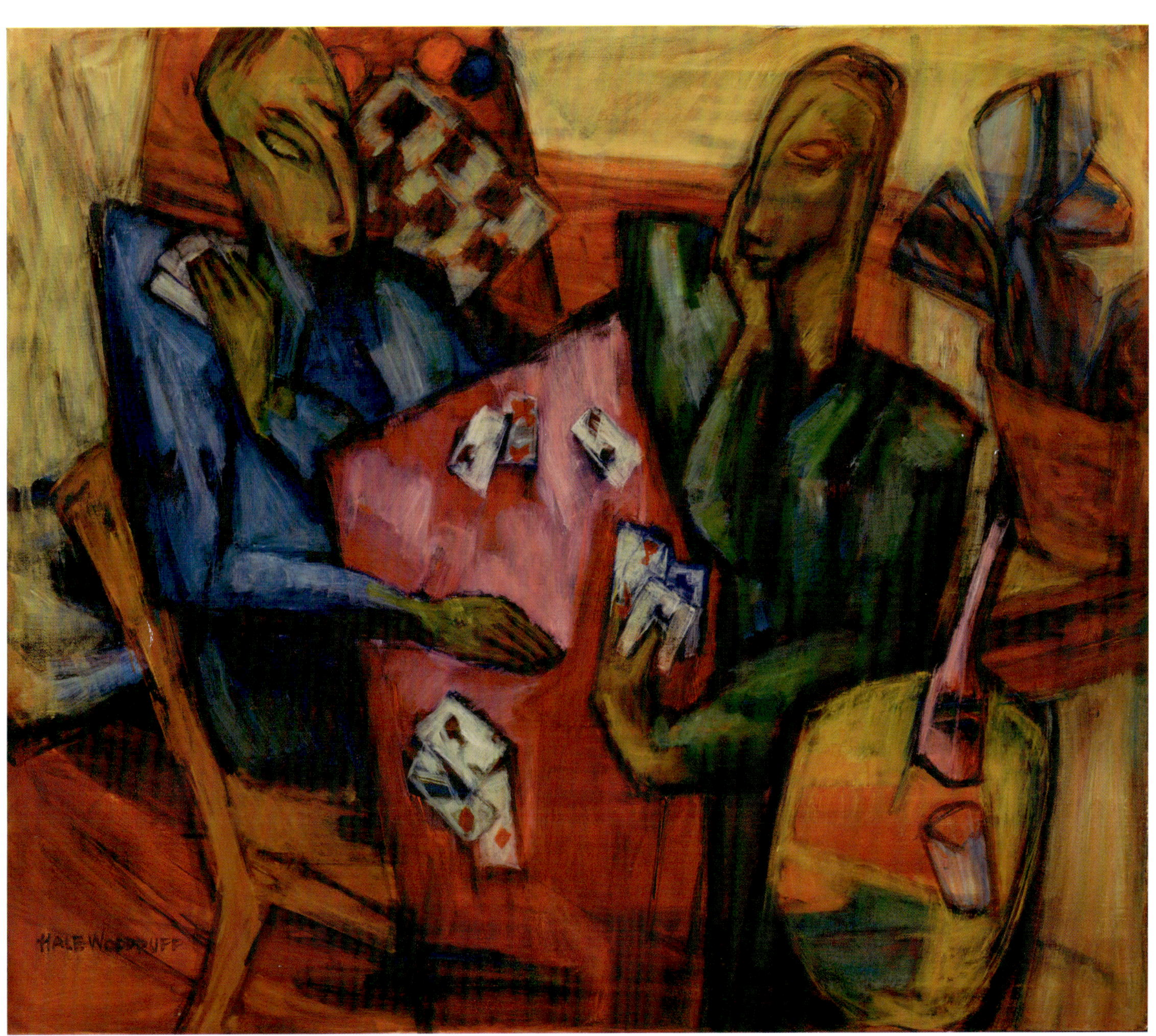
HALE WOODRUFF

HALE A. WOODRUFF

American, 1900–1980

Country Church, 1935

linocut on paper

12 × 12 ¼ in.

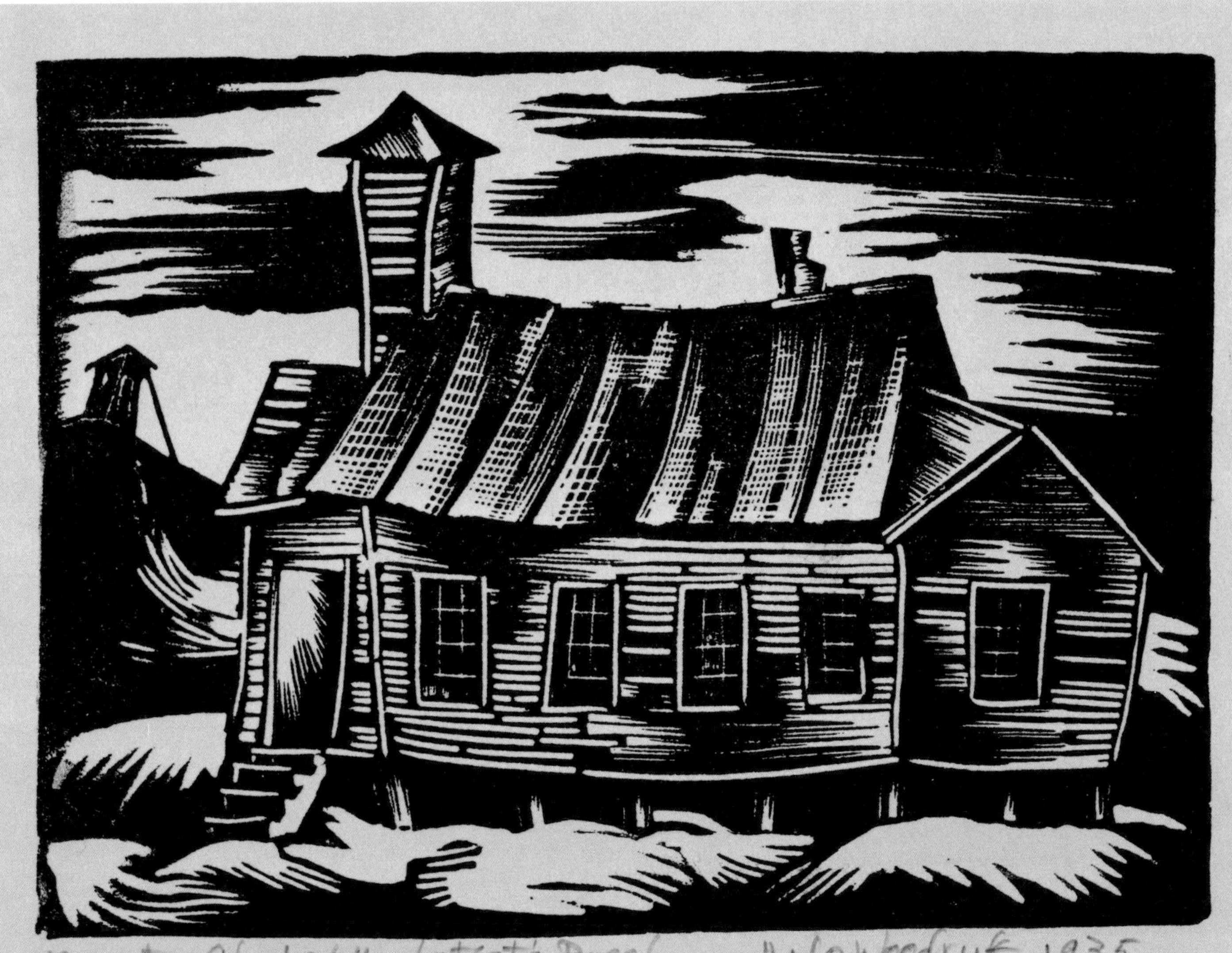
"Country Church" - Artist's Proof - Hale Woodruff - 1935

HALE A. WOODRUFF

American, 1900–1980

Sentinel Gate, 1977

oil on canvas

39 × 29 in.

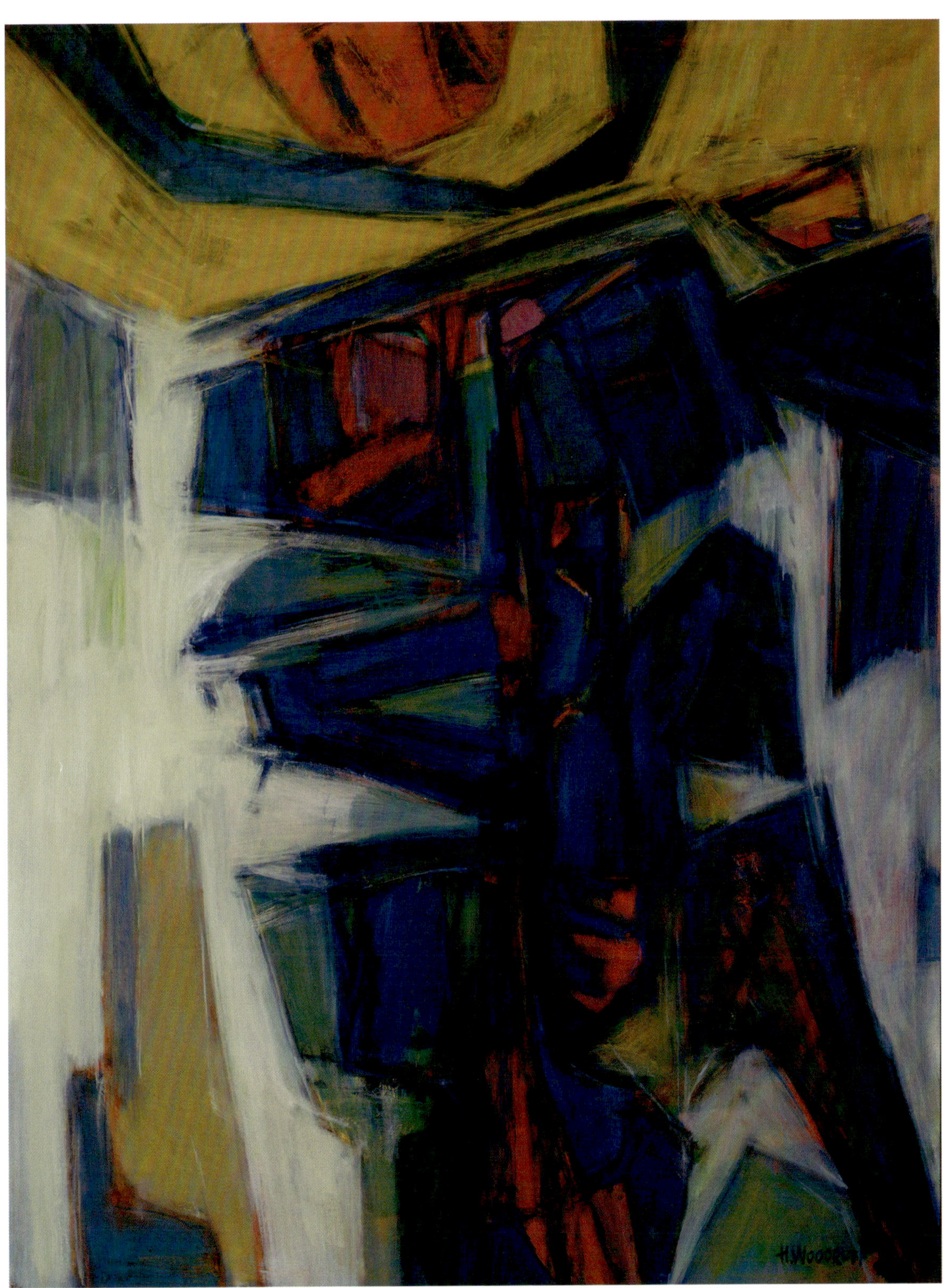

HALE A. WOODRUFF
American, 1900–1980
Two Torsos, c. 1977
charcoal on paper
27 ¾ × 20 in.

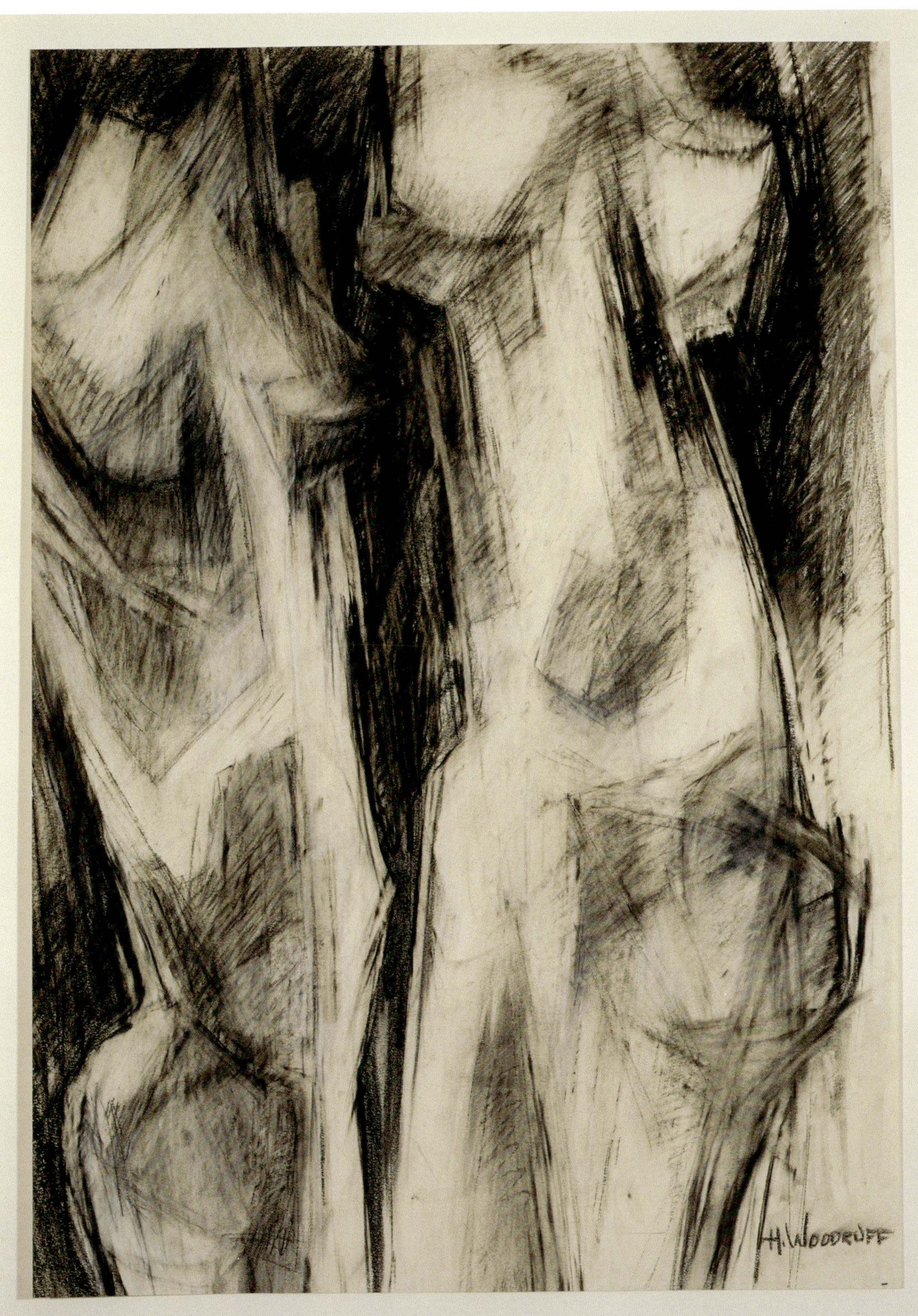
H. WOODRUFF

A PASSION FOR COLLECTING

THE JOHN AND VIVIAN HEWITT STORY

In the summer of 1960, John and Vivian Hewitt bought a painting. It is a bright and gorgeous canvas, bursting with color and featuring the brown and black faces of three Haitian women.

The Hewitts were in Haiti on their second honeymoon, in La Brochette, an artists' colony nestled in a corner of Port-au-Prince, the capital city once described as the Paris of the Caribbean. There, surrounded by the luminous, flamboyant trees, the couple's eyes locked on the colorful canvas. They were drawn to the women because they reflected the rhythm, joie de vivre, and never-say-die spirit that marked the vibrant culture of a people the couple grew to adore.

The Hewitts loved the painting, and it was their first purchase of an original piece of art. It cost forty dollars—money that Vivian Hewitt had earned working overtime as a foundation librarian. Today, the museum-quality painting is valued at four thousand dollars.

Every other year for twenty-five years, the couple would return to Haiti. Each time they left, they would take a little piece of the heart of

Haiti with them. Over the years, they commissioned works and developed friendships with the artists, including such well-known painters as Bernard Séjourné, Luce Turnier, and Luckner Lazard. Eventually, the Hewitts amassed more than three hundred pieces of Haitian art.

While they may have purchased their first original work in Haiti, the couple's deep love of art was evident almost a decade before they ever traveled to the Caribbean nation. In 1949, while on honeymoon in New York City, the couple glided arm-in-arm through the city's museums and galleries, and they wanted to commemorate their special moment with art. Back then, when the newlyweds were making their first art purchases, they could only afford "good prints" and picked up reproductions of still lifes by Picasso, Van Gogh, Orozco, and others.

"Art was cheap and we could afford it. That's how we began," recalled Vivian Hewitt. The art collection began with the acquisition of their first Haitian original painting. But over the next fifty years, it flowered to include some of the most beloved and recognized African American masters: Romare Bearden, Jacob Lawrence, Elizabeth Catlett, and others.

Although they were buying art on a limited budget, they would eventually acquire fine paintings, prints, and drawings, gathering one of the largest and most significant collections of African American art in the nation. The often-rare works are highly valued for their artistic merit and the sweep of the caliber of artists represented in the collection. In 1996, during the Clinton administration, Henry Ossawa Tanner's *Sand Dunes at Sunset, Atlantic City*, became the first work by an African American painter to hang permanently in the White House, and because the Hewitts owned pieces by Tanner, the couple was invited to attend.

Vivian Hewitt told the *Pittsburgh Post-Gazette* in 2011 that gathering the artists' work was akin to "investing in our heritage and culture." Scholar and oral historian Annie Segan says that the Hewitts "saw art collecting as a way of creating a public resource that would educate and engage others to appreciate and collect art." The work in their collection features black families embracing, dark girls in big hats swinging as if reaching for the sky, men building canals, women harvesting, and lovers cuddling at Easter. In their collection are the stories of washerwomen, bluesmen, and card players. What they gathered was hung over nearly every free space in their Upper West Side apartment in New York and represented a broad palette of styles and history. Over time, their life became interwoven with many of the artists as they established friendships and immersed themselves in the New York City's black arts scene.

In the summer of 1958, Vivian Hewitt met and befriended Elizabeth Catlett. Hewitt was in Mexico on assignment with the Rockefeller Foundation when Langston Hughes introduced her to the artist. She would watch Catlett work in her studio. The Hewitts were witness as sculptor, painter, and accomplished printmaker Margaret Burroughs, along with her husband, founded the DuSable Museum of African American History in Chicago. Burroughs was a close friend to John Hewitt's sister, Adele. Through friends, the couple met Hale Woodruff, an art professor who studied in Paris, trained with Diego Rivera, and founded the art department at Atlanta University. Vivian Hewitt's cousin, J. Eugene Grisby, studied under Woodruff at New York University. Grisby would go on to become a noted and in-demand artist as well.

Such social connections and intricate, often class-based networks became important avenues for helping black artists survive. When the Hewitts first began their collecting, many mainstream museums and galleries saw little value in black art and often had no African American artists represented. The Hewitts objected to the absence and decided they could bring visibility to black artists. They often opened their home to serve as a salon, creating a space in which to socialize, educate, and spotlight black artists. The couple had their first salon in 1973, when they invited over fifty friends to raise funding for an artist who wanted to live in Haiti for a year to paint. Over time, they held salons for their artist friends, including Woodruff, Ernie Crichlow, and Bearden. "We were committed to supporting African American artists," Hewitt wrote in her autobiography, "because they were not mainstreamed to the extent that white artists were."

The Hewitts met at Atlanta University in 1949. At the time, in a segregated society, the school's graduate programs were magnets for African American creative, intellectual, and social strivers. It was the gathering ground for "the Talented Tenth"—the educated black population that sociologist W. E. B. Du Bois believed should lead the masses. Vivian Davidson and John Hewitt fit right in.

Vivian Ann Davidson was born in New Castle, a small and close-knit community in western Pennsylvania. In her family home hung a prized painting of a cow pasture, an oil on canvas that first stoked the young girl's love of fine art. She was the fourth of five children. Her mother had been a schoolteacher and her father, a former soldier, served as a butler to the lieutenant governor of Pennsylvania, which Vivian would later state was a dignified profession for a black man in the early part of the twentieth century.

Vivian lived in an integrated ward and walked to integrated schools, where she excelled in art, music, and science. After high school, she majored in French and earned a bachelor's degree from Geneva College in 1943. She went on to earn a master's in library science from the Carnegie Tech Library School, which was later folded into the University of Pittsburgh's School of Information Sciences. She was the first black librarian hired by the Carnegie Library of Pittsburgh and worked in the Hill District and Homewood branches before moving to Atlanta. In her distinguished career, she worked as a resourceful chief librarian for the Rockefeller Foundation, the Carnegie Endowment for International Peace, and the Council on Foreign Relations.

The man Vivian Davidson would marry was equally impressive. She met John Hewitt when he was a humanities dean and English professor at Morehouse College in Atlanta. He became one of the nation's first black medical writers. He was born in 1924, amid the glow of the Harlem Renaissance, into a family that lived in a fourteen-room home in Sugar Hill, a middle-class neighborhood that was the cultural center of a striving, achievement-oriented Harlem.

John had four older half siblings, the youngest of whom, Adele, worked in advertising for the pioneering black newspaper the *Amsterdam News* and later, for many years, served as personal secretary to the internationally renowned poet Langston Hughes. Adele also ran what was known as the Marketplace Art Gallery, a Harlem salon visited by many black intellectuals and artists. Her friend Hughes had his book party there for his novel *Tambourines to Glory*. For John Hewitt, Harlem was an urban academy of arts and culture. He grew up in an atmosphere rich with poets, actors, artists, and scholars. He lived within walking distance of Du Bois, actor and social activist Paul Robeson, and actress Butterfly McQueen.

When it came time for college, John Hewitt studied at Harvard for two years and then returned to New York City, earning his bachelor's and master's degrees at New York University. He then became a reporter for the *People's Voice* and the *Amsterdam News* before leaving for Atlanta to teach English and humanities.

Vivian left Pittsburgh in 1949. She was headed to Atlanta University to work as a librarian and instructor. She met John on September 17, the day after she arrived on campus. They were engaged by Thanksgiving and married on December 26.

A little over a decade later, the couple saw a painting in Haiti. It changed everything and they poured themselves into art collecting, becoming a part of a first generation of African American art collectors. Their passionate investment and dedication to black artists inspired and opened the doors to others interested in collecting and sharing the importance of African American arts. The interviews on the following pages tell some of their stories.

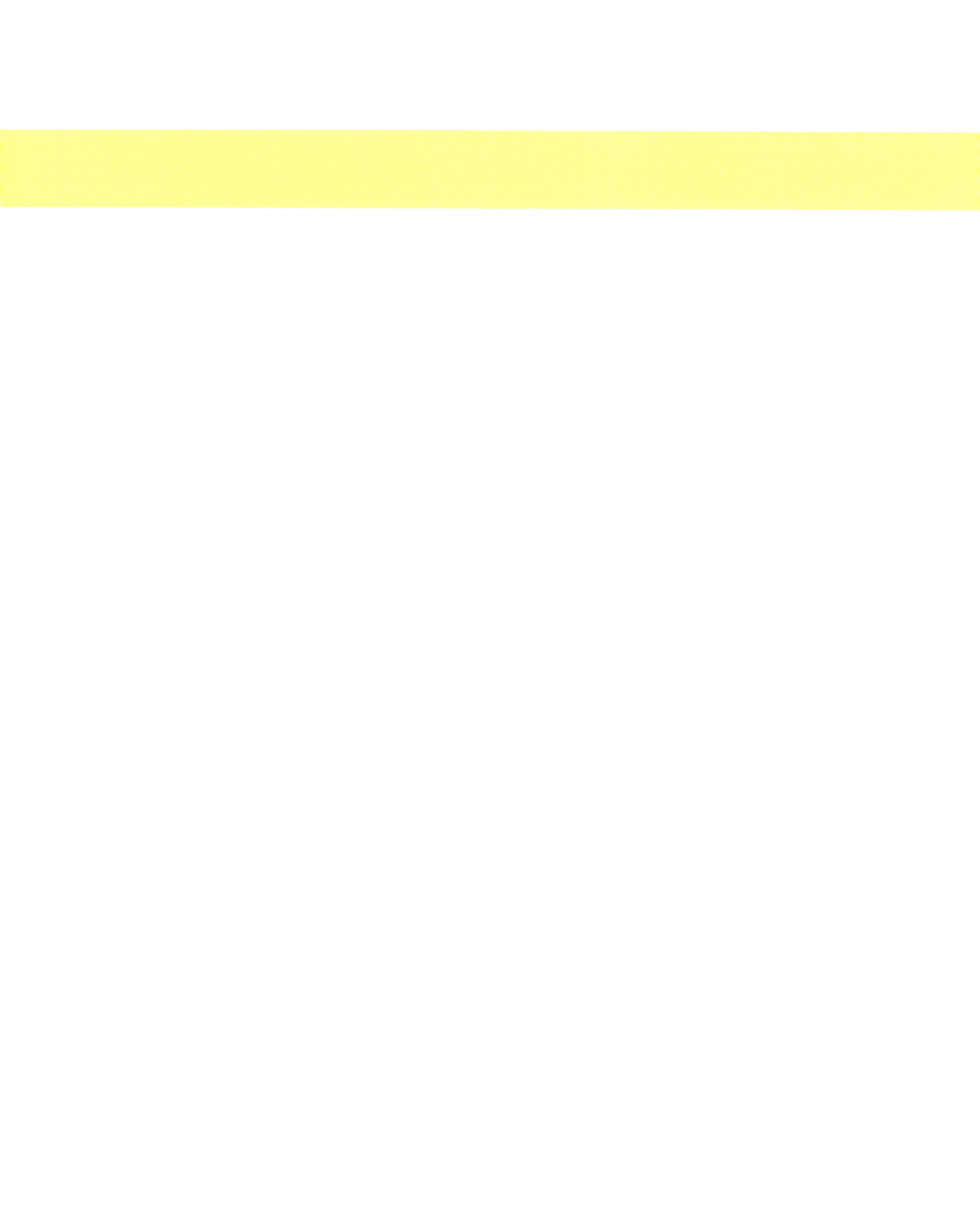

COLLECTORS' PERSPECTIVES

DR. WALTER O. & MRS. LINDA EVANS

In the fall of 1962, a young sailor stationed in Philadelphia went on a date.

At the Philadelphia Museum of Art, the nineteen-year-old was also on his first visit ever to an art museum. As Walter O. Evans strolled through the bright chambers, he was awed by the paintings and sculpture. The excursion changed his life. And, it set in motion a passion and mission that has touched the lives of untold numbers of youth and adults.

Captivated by what he saw, Evans developed a newfound love for art and literature. Over the years, no matter where he lived or traveled Evans was drawn to museums, galleries, and libraries. Even as he studied at Howard University and the University of Michigan Medical School, educating himself about art and artists also became his focus.

Whether in Europe or America, Evans continued to notice that there was little if any African American art in museum collections. In the late 1970s, while he was working as a surgeon in Detroit, Evans had an encounter with a friend, an educator and artist who managed a local gallery. Based on her recommendation, he purchased Jacob Lawrence's *The Legend of John Brown*, a portfolio of twenty-two silkscreen prints. It was his first acquisition of major art.

Over the next three decades, Walter Evans and his wife, Linda, built a private collection of more than five hundred original pieces, including paintings, sculptures, and photographs by African American artists. The collection dates from 1848 to more contemporary pieces and includes such master African American artists as Robert S. Duncanson, Edmonia Lewis, and the Harlem Renaissance's Aaron Douglas.

While Evans was building a significant art collection, he continued to educate himself and to be enthralled. He would go from reading about the artists in hushed rooms in a library to befriending them, hosting them in his home, inviting them to lectures in Detroit, and eventually commissioning them to produce works of art. Evans came to know Romare Bearden, Jacob Lawrence, Elizabeth Catlett, photographer Gordon Parks, and others.

When he retired from surgical practice in Detroit in June 2001, Evans went home to Savannah, Georgia, the city on the river where he was born. Today, in the same city where segregation once blocked many of its citizens from visiting local museums, Evans's passion for art is opening doors for all children to learn about and enjoy the art he didn't get a chance to see as a child.

Evans has donated seventy pieces of his varied collection of African American art to the Savannah College of Art and Design. The collection will be housed in a gallery renovated from an old train depot that was originally constructed by enslaved men, who even made the bricks for the building. Evans's mother was born near the depot, which will now bear her son's name as the Walter O. Evans Center for African American Studies. Along with studios, classrooms, and educational programming, the center leverages the Evans collection and will provide a wider lens to study African American art.

As a remarkable legacy is built and efforts to magnify appreciation for African American art increase, Evans hasn't forgotten the youngest patrons. One of Evans's stipulations in gifting the collection was that schoolchildren be admitted to the center for free. "Museums and their collections," Evans said, "are like windows into life and culture. I wanted to make sure that children were able to visit and not miss out."

Using his collection as a tool for education—a living legacy—was also a concern of Evans's. For sixteen years, part of the extensive collection has been on tour in about fifty cities. Walter and Linda Evans have established the Walter O. Evans Foundation for Art and Literature to ensure the collection will continue to serve as a resource. His aim, Evans says, is to make sure that every child has the opportunity to learn from the artwork and to see themselves and their history reflected on gallery walls.

When Evans was an emerging collector, acquiring black art wasn't as popular as it is today. Today, African American art has increased in value, but collecting it isn't a new practice. His advice to others desiring to build their own collections: purchase what you like and enjoy, research the artist, and get experts to evaluate the artwork.

COLLECTORS' PERSPECTIVES

DR. HARMON & MRS. HARRIET KELLEY

The couple came late to art collecting. When they began, they were both over thirty years old, raising their two daughters, establishing careers, and engaging in community work. They had some catching up to do.

Dr. Harmon Kelley and his wife, Harriet, enlisted supportive, knowledgeable dealers who led them by the hand. One such dealer was Thurlow Tibbs, an African American collector who began with paintings bequeathed to him by his grandmother, Lillian Evans Tibbs, one of the first black women to sing opera in Europe.

Once the Kelleys' collection began to blossom, they committed themselves to studying the artists represented among their acquisitions, learning their backstories and the techniques that each used to make their art shine. Soon, the Kelleys' collection of African American art—which included such masterful painters as Robert S. Duncanson, Edward Mitchell Bannister, Edmonia Lewis, Archibald Motley, and Jacob Lawrence—began to travel. And they went with it. They zigzagged across much of the

United States, lecturing on the artwork and sharing their joy of collecting.

The couple crossed the waters, too, timing their vacations in the capitals of Europe to coincide with must-see art exhibitions. One such journey to London was especially sweet. It was the late 1990s, and Harmon and Harriet Kelley were in Great Britain for *Rhapsodies in Black: Art of the Harlem Renaissance*, an exhibition meant to showcase the expanded definition and culture of what it means to be a part of the African diaspora. One morning, Harriet Kelley woke to read the *Times* of London. On the front page was an article heralding the impact of the exhibition. It was accompanied by a photograph of the oil painting *Girl in a Red Dress*, by Charles Alston. Mrs. Kelley smiled. The couple owns the painting, and it is one of her favorites.

The Kelleys began acquiring black art and collecting in 1986. Invited to the San Antonio exhibition *Hidden Heritage: Afro-American Art, 1800–1950*, the couple was "blown away" by the work of then such little-known artists as Lawrence, Romare Bearden, and Elizabeth Catlett. They returned to the show again and again and again, each time becoming absorbed deeper into the stories and emotions laid across the canvases. What they saw inspired their first purchase of a work by a black artist: *The Visitor*, a 1910 pastel by Henry Ossawa Tanner. They went on to learn more about collecting and began to acquire landscapes and portraits to hang on the walls of their new home.

Today, the Kelleys own hundreds of pieces, making their African American art collection one of the most impressive in the world. In 1995, 150 pieces became the first private collection of black American art ever exhibited by the Smithsonian Institution in Washington, DC.

Speaking with Harriet Kelley is like conversing with an art historian. As her family's collection grew, so did her intimate knowledge of individual artists—through personal friendship with the artists, because she studied catalogues and pored over their biographies, and because she researched their pasts.

Collecting African American art today is more challenging than it was when they began, says Mrs. Kelley. For one, the value of the art is better recognized, which means that such art will cost more to acquire, particularly historical works and those by artists connected to the Harlem Renaissance. She suggests that nascent collectors begin with what they love, that they invest in contemporary art, find up-and-coming artists, and even begin to follow and support the art of college and high school students. Also, she suggests that developing relationships with dealers and artists can have positive outcomes. Mrs. Kelley says that her family was able to acquire *The Artist's Wife*—a much-sought-after portrait done in 1936 by artist Horace Pippin—because the dealer allowed the Kelleys to pay in installments.

"It's important to collect," says Harriet Kelley, "because it helps to preserve the culture and history and it helps the artists." At one point, to save money, many black artists had to reuse their canvases. On the back of one of their Tanner canvases, the Kelleys discovered that the artist had painted a portrait of his son.

In recent years Mrs. Kelley has also begun to collect works on paper. She has a collection of seventy images, which has toured in Seattle and Houston and is planned for museums across the country.

The Kelleys see the collection as an education—for themselves and for others. Ernie Crichlow's *The Lovers* depicts a Klansman hovering over a young black girl and bespeaks racial prejudice and sexual dominance; John Wilson's *Streetcar Scene* tells a story of segregation as a proud black worker wearing his union pin is ignored by passengers on the bus.

"The collection," says Harriet Kelley, "tells of the lives of African Americans and has the power to negate the stereotypes of blacks as being lazy and shiftless." She adds, "When people see these images, they see the everyday life of African Americans," and "people come away giving these matters a lot of thought. It's art that educates blacks and whites as well."

In a recent exhibition at Reynolda Village in Winston-Salem, North Carolina, a Bannister farm scene that the Kelleys had gifted to the San Antonio museum was on loan to help tell the story of American farm life and identity. "We're proud to see museums are being inclusive and using black art to tell the whole American story," she says. "This is what should be done and is being done."

For the Kelleys, art also is healing. In 2006, Mr. Kelley's father died. In the midst of Mrs. Kelley's grief for her father-in-law, she became seriously ill. One thing that aided her recovery was preparation for a lecture on the collection. The constant review of her art was restorative, giving her a sense of pride, courage, and strength—the same character traits she imagined the black artists would have needed to draw upon to create, and the same stories and themes reflected in much of the art they crafted. In many ways, says Harriet Kelley, "art has been my therapy."

COLLECTORS' PERSPECTIVES

FROM AN INTERVIEW WITH NANCY WASHINGTON

A handkerchief hangs in Nancy Washington's bathroom. The framed piece, *Woman Standing by Trees*, is small, slightly larger than seven inches square. But the pale, gossamer-like lithograph on fabric is compelling.

Nancy Washington and her husband, Milton, purchased the artwork in the early 1980s in Atlanta. Mrs. Washington describes the piece as beautiful and delicate. But that's only a part of what she sees and what the artist intended. The slight cloth is a powerful work by Betye Saar, an African American whose art challenges racial and gendered caricatures and stereotypes. Saar has been described as an artist who uses her creations to give voice to political and social protest. She once said that her work turns a "negative, demeaning figure into a positive, empowered" statement. Saar's handkerchief is no exception. It turns an object frequently used to negatively depict African American women as domestics into a work of art that Mrs. Washington is now able to call "beautiful."

In the lower left-hand corner of the lacy kerchief, an African American woman is shrouded in a violet shadow. The image, perhaps from the early 1900s, shows a well-dressed woman standing tall in a wide-brimmed hat. Looking self-assuredly forward, she is a symbol of pride. In fact, Saar's art and its ability to turn defeat into dignity is precisely what appealed to the Washingtons.

The Washingtons have been collecting for about four decades, about the same amount of time that they've made their home in Pittsburgh, where they became known for their dedication and service to the city's civic, business, educational, and cultural advancements. When the couple first married, they collected mostly posters, but over the years they have acquired some ninety pieces of original African American art. Saar's handkerchief, one of the first original works of art the Washingtons purchased, remains beloved.

They couple collects drawings, etchings, paintings, and photography of and by African Americans. That is their focus. The art in their collection spans 170 years, from early African American artists such as Robert S. Duncanson and Edward Mitchell Bannister to contemporary artists such as Lorna Simpson and Willie Cole. While it is an expansive collection, all of the art shares a common thread—the ability to evoke a spirited feeling of success.

"Everyone says to us, 'Surely you have Jacob Lawrence?' And we don't. We don't collect the struggle. We collect the triumph. And it's our choice. And it's what we want to surround ourselves with," says Mrs. Washington, "but it is not a denial of the struggle."

Asking when they began enjoying art "is like asking, 'When did you have your first glass of water?'" says Nancy Washington. There is no beginning, she says; enjoying and being around art has always been part of who they are. Mrs. Washington's father was a trailblazing educator. In 1953, he was the first African American to be district superintendent of the Philadelphia public schools. When he got together with his friends, they didn't play games or dribble a ball; they drew. Through her father, Mrs. Washington is also related to the distinguished artist Henry Ossawa Tanner, the first African American artist to have a painting to hang permanently in the White House. Mrs. Washington was an adult, living in Pittsburgh, where Tanner was born, when the US government released a stamp to commemorate his legacy to art. That's when she first realized Tanner's distinction as an American artist.

For the Washingtons, the "why" of collecting is the more important question. The couple collects because it is a way of chronicling the history of a community of people that traverses centuries and generations. It's also a way of seeing their stories as they saw the world. "When you surround yourself with these stories, they enrich your life and they become a part of your life, and you are always grounded in this context of where you come from and who you are," says Mrs. Washington. "This shapes our identity as Americans and African Americans."

She goes on to add: "We collect because we want to remember. We want to remember the people of our community and nation who, at many different times and in many different places, struggled so that all could see the world as they saw it. Through their eyes and with their hands, they gave us the smiles of their companions, the exuberance of their entertainers, and the sometimes loneliness of their spirits. Over the years, we have gotten to meet some of the artists and heard their stories through long conversations. We remember all of this as we look at their work in the world on our walls, and we call them our friends."

The Washingtons' joy as longtime collectors has also come from connecting with a community of collectors. It's an effort that keeps them in touch with artists as well as people, past and present, who helped to cultivate art and black art collecting. In the 1990s the couple was able to meet artist Thurlow Tibbs, a groundbreaking dealer whose mother had been a collector of older black artists. Tibbs was selling a few pieces and the Washingtons were ready and able to purchase a number of works from him. Around the same time, the couple met Isobel Neal, a pioneering Chicago gallery owner who curated shows of quality black art. They purchased photo etchings by Roy DeCarava from Neal's gallery.

Vivian Hewitt was another "amazing woman" in the community of collectors. Mrs. Washington describes Hewitt as a "godmother" who is focused on the art of collecting and helping people to get to know artists and their work so that collectors can get the pieces they love. "She is like the light," says Mrs. Washington. Furthermore, she says, once people know you're collecting, they find you. Closer to home, Richard Armstrong, once the director of the Carnegie Museum of Art in Pittsburgh, was very helpful to the Washingtons' collection efforts. The couple traveled with him to Switzerland and Miami where they acquired new pieces for their growing collection. Support also came from Lynn Zelevansky, the Henry J. Heinz II Director of the Carnegie Museum of Art.

For Mrs. Washington, calling one piece or another her favorite often changes from day to day. Currently, the object of her adoration is a photograph by Malick Sidibé of two young people dancing in Mali. "There is something about the expressions on their faces . . . their bodies. It just makes me smile every time I walk by it. It's so beautiful."

THE COLLECTION

THE HARVEY B. GANTT CENTER FOR AFRICAN-AMERICAN ARTS + CULTURE & THE JOHN & VIVIAN HEWITT COLLECTION OF AFRICAN-AMERICAN ART

We bought each of those pieces because we loved them;
they were a part of our lives.

—VIVIAN DAVIDSON HEWITT

John and Vivian Hewitt purchased their first work of art—a reproduction of a Picasso—on their honeymoon in 1949 in New York City. This first buy grew to include original works of art given to each other as gifts for birthdays and anniversaries, a more focused collection of Haitian art, and ultimately, fifty-eight two-dimensional works selected and acquired by Bank of America in 1998 and pledged to what was then the Afro-American Cultural Center.

After traveling to over twenty-five museums across the country, the John and Vivian Hewitt Collection of African-American Art returned to its new home, the Harvey B. Gantt Center, an award-winning structure built in 2009 to present, preserve, and celebrate excellence in the art, history, and culture of African Americans and others of African descent. Bank of America's generous gift became the cornerstone of the Gantt Center's permanent collection and presented the masters—among them Romare Bearden, Elizabeth Catlett, Jacob Lawrence, Henry Ossawa Tanner, and Hale Woodruff—to art enthusiasts, first-time museumgoers, and students throughout the southeastern United States.

This significant gift, coupled with strong exhibitions featuring today's masters like Sam Gilliam, Malick Sidibé, and Jonathan Green and mid-career makers like María Magdalena Campos-Pons and Radcliffe Bailey, has helped to elevate the Gantt Center to a leading role among African American arts institutions. Because the Gantt Center's permanent holdings now include oil paintings by Tanner and Woodruff and charcoal drawings by John Biggers, other art collectors have begun to donate works. A coveted Bearden collage and a mixed-media sculpture by emerging artist Leonardo Benzant have made their way into the collection. In addition, the Hewitts' legacy of collecting has led the Gantt Center to chart a bold course in the acquisition of new works.

We at the Gantt Center believe education and public programs are integral to the success of our institution, and we established the Hewitt Education Fund in the couple's honor to support programming that heightens appreciation of the Hewitt Collection and other Gantt Center exhibitions. This fund also fosters opportunities for lifelong learning.

Continuing the work begun by the Hewitts when they graciously opened their home to provide a space for artists to share their work more broadly, the Hewitt Education Fund increases access to the arts by supporting key initiatives such as the Gantt Center's Community Arts Project, which links artists with local communities. These artists collaborate with residents to define the scale and scope of a project and then create public artworks that remain in the partner neighborhood. In 2010, in lieu of gifts for her ninetieth birthday, Mrs. Hewitt invited friends and colleagues to contribute to the fund.

Ever our advocate, Mrs. Hewitt met privately with a group of twenty Gantt Center donors and trustees when we last exhibited the collection in Charlotte, North Carolina. She encouraged them to support African American artists and African American art institutions in general, and the Harvey B. Gantt Center in particular, challenging us all to do more. She reminded us that "art enhances, enriches, and expands one's life."

In 2013, photographic images of the fifty-eight works that make up the John and Vivian Hewitt Collection were launched in a virtual gallery on the Gantt Center website. A video of Mrs. Hewitt introduces the collection, and the virtual gallery provides descriptions of the works and biographical sketches of the artists. Casual viewers, artists, educators, and students alike are now able to explore the collection and the artists in greater detail, thereby expanding its reach globally.

Digitizing the Hewitt Collection was important to both the Gantt Center and to Mrs. Hewitt. When they chose to sell the collection, the Hewitts voiced their desire to have the works remain together to serve "as an educational tool that would inspire other collectors—to show that you did not have to be rich to invest in art—and to introduce young people to marvelous artists who just happen to be African American."

This array of paintings, drawings, prints, and collages has grown in value because of its richness and its lessons. Beyond the magnificent works themselves and the artists who created them, the collection teaches us about supporting artists and collecting, and about the collectors. The opportunity to now present this highly acclaimed assemblage to the Pittsburgh community—a place dear to Vivian Hewitt—stands as a testament to the power of a vision, the one shared by a young couple honeymooning in New York almost seventy years ago.

DAVID R. TAYLOR
President and CEO
Harvey B. Gantt Center for African-American Arts + Culture

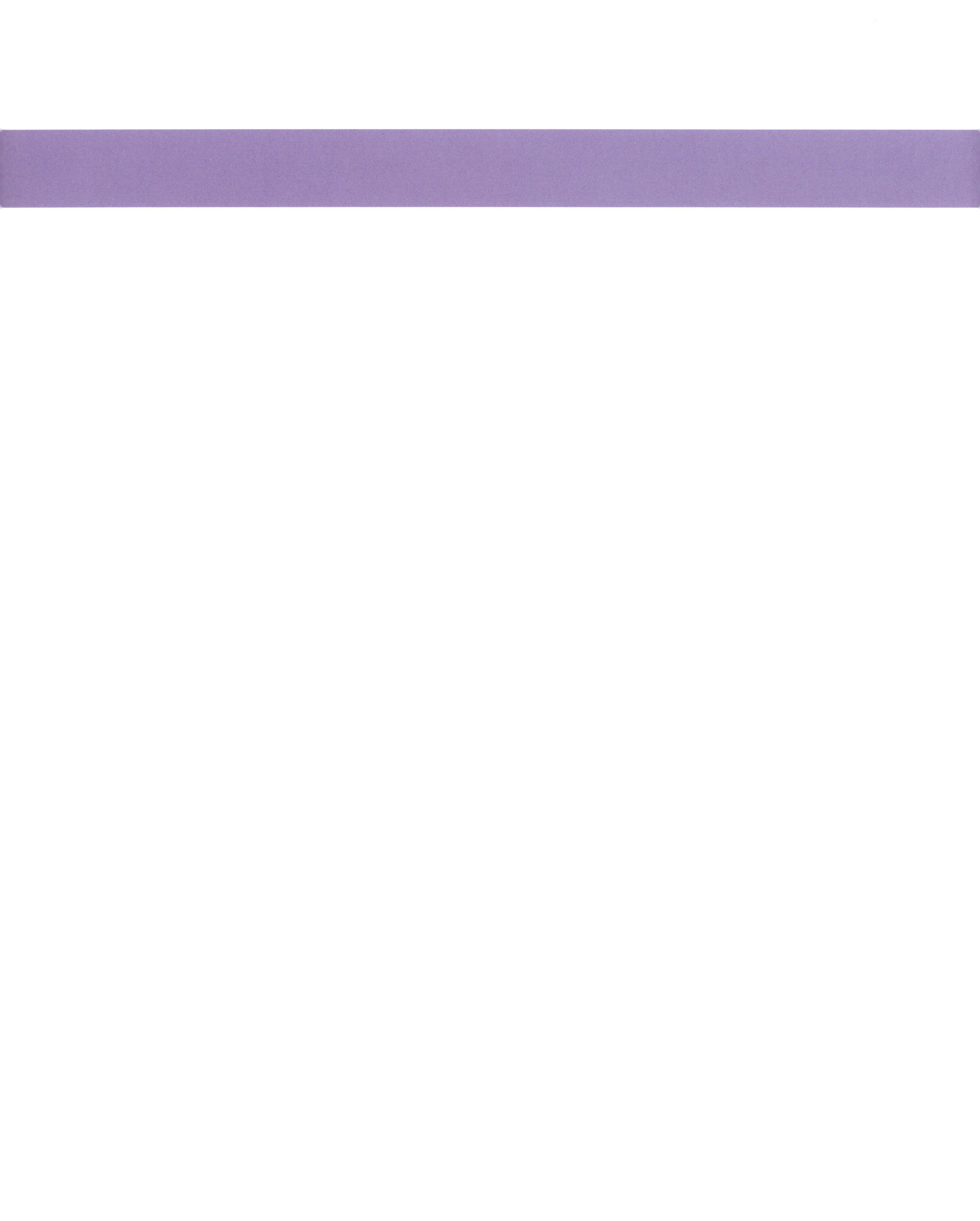

ART PERMISSIONS

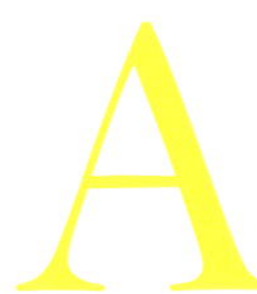
ll images courtesy of The Harvey B. Gantt Canter for African-American Arts + Culture. The John and Vivan Hewitt Collection of African-American Art was generously donated by Bank of America.

Every effort has been made to contact and acknowledge copyright holders for all reproductions; additional rights holders are encouraged to contact the Harvey B. Gantt Center for African-American Arts + Culture, 551 South Tryon Street, Charlotte, NC 28202.

Romare Bearden: Art © Romare Bearden Foundation / Licensed by VAGA, New York, NY

John T. Biggers: Art © John T. Biggers Estate / Licensed by VAGA, New York, NY

Margaret Burroughs: Art Courtesy Eric Toller

Elizabeth Catlett: Art © Catlett Mora Family Trust / Licensed by VAGA, New York, NY

James Denmark: Art © James Denmark

Jonathan Green: Art © Special Permission from Artist Jonathan Green

J. Eugene Grigsby: Art © Special Permission from the Estate of Artist J. Eugene Grigsby

Alvin C. Hollingsworth: Art Courtesy Mrs. Margery Hollingsworth Mitchell

Jacob Lawrence: Art © 2016, The Jacob and Gwendolyn Lawrence Foundation, Seattle / Artists Rights Society (ARS), New York

Hughie Lee-Smith: Art © Estate of Hughie Lee-Smith / Licensed by VAGA, New York, NY

Virginia Evans Smit: Art © The Harvey B. Gantt Center for African-American Arts + Culture

Ann Tanksley: Art © Special Permission from Artist Ann Tanksley

Frank Wimberly: Art © Frank W. Wimberly

Hale A. Woodruff: Art © Estate of Hale Woodruff / Licensed by VAGA, New York, NY